TORN BACK AND RAW

TORN BACK AND RAW

An Intimate Portrayal of a
Life Hijacked by Mental Illness

JOHANNA STENERSEN

LUMINARE PRESS
WWW.LUMINAREPRESS.COM

Printed in the United States of America

Luminare Press
442 Charnelton St.
Eugene, OR 97401
www.luminarepress.com

LCCN: 2021915956
ISBN: 978-1-64388-709-8

*I dedicate this book
to all of the beautiful, innocent souls,
victims of trauma and mental illness who have
suffered in silence and suffered alone…
I hear you, and I'm sorry for your
pain and suffering*

CONTENTS

CHAPTER 1

Motorcycles Saved My Life

One of my greatest joys and achievements while growing up was my talent for riding motorcycles. Influenced by my brother and his friends, I learned quickly and easily how to ride, and ride I did behind our home in San Clemente, California, along rolling hills and narrow trails bordered mostly with the dense, brilliant beauty of wild mustard weeds.

From the time I returned home from school to the setting of the sun, I rode in those hills. To me, riding motorcycles was like being given wings and taught to fly—it bought me freedom from the chaos and unpredictability of home. It was exhilarating, challenging, and fun, and soon it became my passion and my refuge. I discovered life, love of nature, and solace riding in those hills.

At age thirteen, I began competing and continued until I was nineteen. Winning at racing soon earned much of what I did not get at home: attention and praise. It also gave me confidence in my physical and athletic abilities. I am so grateful to have had such a positive outlet, emotionally, physically, and spiritually, that those years of riding and racing provided me. Thank you, Divine Creator, for your loving and timely provision. You knew exactly what this lost and angry little girl needed back then to successfully navigate through the difficult and painful terrain of her childhood. I will be forever thankful.

CHAPTER 2

I'm Telling My Story, My Truth.
The Good. The Bad. The Ugly.

'───

've told no one this story—the shame, anger, and fear I've carried my entire life kept me retreating from people. I struggled and suffered alone.

Let me say upfront that I loved my parents, and they were really, really good people, but as parents, they were better suited to parenting goldfish.

Occupied with her own problems, my mom was easily provoked to jealousy, convinced my dad was cheating on her—always that same theme, just played out in different scenarios. Dad worked long hours, which could be suspect but not because he was chasing other women. My father was chasing the "American Dream" so that my mother could have nice things. She always had the very nicest things. Us kids too.

My mother was a beautiful Italian woman—insecure, not educated, and vain about her appearance. I'm told that while carrying me, she starved herself, because she did not want to gain the weight she gained with my brother and oldest sister, Linda. When I was born, you could see the tiny, blue veins through opaque skin. My weight was normal, but I must have looked terribly fragile or sickly, because nobody wanted to hold me. In addition to starving the life out of a tiny, developing brain, my mother's aversion to pain led her to consume a fifth of vodka prior to going into delivery. Whether she drank during her pregnancy or not, I don't know. My guess is that she did.

My father, a farm boy from Montana, hitchhiked to California with two quarters in his pocket and the clothes on his back. His education came from his time in the Air Force. He met and married my mom following World War II and discovered early that he had a lot to prove to both sides of the family. Dad came from a family of strong, educated, and accomplished women. His mother, an educator and mean as a snake, beat him at whim continually throughout his young life for no apparent reason.

His sister, Elnora, was thirteen months older, brilliant, talented, athletic, and competitive. He followed in her shadow. Expectations from family and teachers to be like Elnora became too great, forcing him to run like hell from Montana at the first chance. Elnora was also an educator with several doctoral degrees. As a professor at the University of Missoula, one of her assignments was to live among the natives, learn their language, write it, and get it in print so everyone had an opportunity to read and learn the stories passed down from generations. Elnora was also responsible for getting the first native into university, and she was the last of the true humanitarians.

Other family members included two older brothers, two younger sisters, and his father, all of whom he never spoke much about. Driven, talented, and successful in his own right, my dad was a master cabinet maker with real estate as a hobby, buying up beachfront property in San Clemente. He bought fixer-uppers and turned them into summer rentals. This began in the 1970s. A favorite rental of mine, two streets up from the pier, was a group of eight apartments called the Breakers. We stayed there often during the winter months, and that was pretty cool.

While at the Breakers, my brother, Don, who was quick to fall heir to things, found an empty room the size of a broom closet on ground level. Immediately seeing its potential, he claimed it and converted it into a bachelor pad that consisted of a bed the size of a camp cot and maybe a refrigerator. It was a big deal to a high school kid and surf fanatic to be only a few steps from the beach.

The rental that broke my heart when it sold around 2010 sat three or four streets up from the pier. It might have been called the Panorama, or maybe that's what I recall about it. It was three or four stories up and had a panoramic view of the Pacific Ocean, but more than that, it was the last rental to go and the only one with my dad's skillful fingerprints throughout. I was age thirteen or fourteen the first time Dad brought me there. I was so awed by his beautiful cabinet work, the expanse of the living room, and of course the view and location that I asked him if I could have it when he went to heaven. He responded, "I thought you liked unit #1A." Unit #1A was a dingy, little one-bedroom hovel on the ground level with no windows and no view. Both were sold.

With long hours and hard work, my father succeeded at grabbing ahold of the American Dream, proving that he was indeed "someone," just not someone to be counted on by his kids when we needed him most. Predictably unpredictable is what my father became to me. To his credit, however, he was a great provider. Bad for us, as that's where his parenting responsibilities ended.

CHAPTER 3

My Parents Were Drinkers, Ragers, and Fighters; My Dad, a Hitter

S aid another way, my parents were raging imbeciles when they drank, which was daily, arguing and shouting, yelling obscenities, teasing and taunting and provoking each other like children. My mom would provoke my dad until he completely lost it. That's when the slugging and hair pulling began. My brother, sister, and I watched, alone without comfort and likely frightened to hysteria. Visiting my mom in the hospital the following day with my father was always confusing. Oftentimes dinners would get interrupted by a similar scenario; add dinner plates with food and full beer mugs flying over our heads, exploding loudly into the wood-paneled wall in a room off the kitchen called the rumpus room, thus leaving another battle scar to be reminded of the event.

At Home but Homeless, I Am an Orphan

A memory that returns, again and again, is of my tiny siblings and I huddled together in my oldest sister's room upstairs. We were alone while downstairs the nightmare ensued, foisting upon the wild and frightened imaginations of tiny children whose only clues as to what was happening came from the cacophony of loud noises downstairs that carried warnings of danger! On this night, there was shouting and arguing and things crashing and breaking while at a distance I heard sirens becoming increasingly louder, then the front door slamming open and more voices shouting, one of which was my mother's, yelling she had been raped by my father and to arrest him! All the while she was drunk to the gills and naked. Yeah, boy, good times at the Stenersen casa!

We looked like every other middle-class family on the outside. On the inside, my parents all too often turned our home into a war zone—a harsh, volatile, chaotic space where no tiny human being with its tiny developing brain should ever go. Bad things happen. Wires get crossed and short circuit, synapses fire amiss, brain chemistry gets altered, the nervous system gets jacked, and BAM! A serial killer is born!! While I did not become a serial killer (not for a lack of homicidal thoughts), what I got was a whole lot of heartache, anguish, and challenges often too great to bear alone. I was always alone.

CHAPTER 4

The Best Years of My Life
1969–1978

R iding motorcycles...that was a new frontier and a world demanding exploration. This drew the athlete out in me as well as the competitor. I was smart, determined, and driven. At around age sixteen, a friend got me a job at Nautilus Fitness of Newport Beach, and that's when I began strength training and conditioning. Intrinsically motivated, I trained like crazy, loving every minute because it was what I craved—body, mind, and soul.

In 1975, when I came on the District 37 motocross racing scene at Carlsbad Raceway, I'm not sure I came with any expectations except to ride fast and beat whoever was in front of me. From that day forward, that proved to be a girl named Sue Fish. In addition to Sue being my fiercest rival, we became inseparable friends off the track. Wherever we went together, we always had fun, the silly, mischievous kind of fun that didn't get you killed.

Once Sue and I, all stealth like, got into Irwindale Raceway with a gallon jug of Tyrolia wine under a jacket slung over my shoulder. We were young girls with crushes on hot guys with nice butts like Rod Stewart, David Bowie, and Speedway Hottie, Bruce Penhall (aka Juicy Bruce).

Here we were, feeling good, laughing and being silly idiots up in the bleachers on a cold evening, when Sue and another friend, Marsha Holley, dared me to go down onto the track, grab ahold of Bruce's heinie, which was on display in fitted leathers while straddling his bike, and give a squeeze. Oh yes, I did! How I got from the top of the bleachers to the bottom, over a four-foot wall and onto the red clay oval racetrack as buzzed as I was, is a miracle and a mystery.

There I was, standing behind this blond-haired, blue-eyed, gorgeous, surfer-like hunk (he played a motorcycle CHP in the TV series *CHiPs*) with my hands squeezing his booty, and I howled in absolute glee!

I never considered the possibility that anything could go wrong such as getting tripped up on my assent over the wall and landing face-first on the ground. That would be a crowd pleaser for sure, deserving to be both cheered and booed. What I recalled, thankfully, was the crowd in the grandstands roaring.

Training took on a whole new level of focus and intensity. Fish became the object of my motivation—equally matched, athletic, and driven. Visualizing the face of Fish, usually helped to eke out another rep or two in the gym. I loved the exhilaration I felt from racing and the risk factor as well as the challenge, mentally and physically. It was exactly what I needed at that time. Racing became my passion, my joy, and my drug—it became my lifeline. Along with the pleasure motorcycles gave me came a sizable chip on my shoulder. Deep down I was one pissed-off little girl whose emotional needs and need for parenting largely went unmet, leaving me feeling deeply flawed and ill prepared to engage in life.

> *"I don't want the world to see me,*
> *'cause I don't think that they'd understand*
> *when everything's made to be broken,*
> *I just want you to know who I am"*
>
> —*"Iris," Goo Goo Dolls*

CHAPTER 5

All This Brokenness Inside Me That I Was Not Born With

W hat first became apparent was anxiety, the kind associated with an emotional event or a memory that causes fear and dread, then specifically anxiety regarding math. I would mix up numbers like people with dyslexia mix up letters all the time! It became most apparent when I started college. Math tests with their time restraints threw me into a panic, making concentration impossible. Often the resulting frustration would lead me on a tour in my head (not a good place to spend time!) where I'd find all the reasons to be angry and self-loathing. I was incredibly hard on myself for feeling like an idiot. Add the jackass seated behind me (there was always at least one!), tapping his pencil on his desktop, whose teeth I wanted to smash with my elbow because he was irritating the hell out of me! Not understanding any of this, the confusion I felt overwhelmed me and turned to panic, and I wanted to run.

I have such a terrible fear of failure and so much shame for not being smarter, I am crippled by self-loathing and anger. This anger, reactive and volatile, is always directed at myself and then others unfortunate enough to enter my orbit. I am so defensive, spring-loaded, and ready to launch at the slightest provocation or annoyance.

Big Pain Equals Big Anger

As the weight of all this crazy thinking continues, it drags me down emotionally and physically. Criticism, self-inflected, shamelessly takes its toll on me. The feeling that overtakes me is desperation, needing to get out from under its weight. Sometimes it feels heavy like a wet wool blanket; it always has a way of making me feel so miserable. What a destructive blow criticism is to a self-esteem already pummeled by a lifetime of criticism. The shame I feel burns in the pit of my stomach like a smoldering coal. There is no help. No one to rescue me. *I feel helpless, and I feel despair.* Having been here so often before, I wince at the familiarity. The loss of control frightens me, and my fear quickly turns to anger.

When the craziness does run its course, things turn instinctual, and the all-consuming need to fight or flee kicks in. This has meant angry outbursts, volatile reactions, and a limited ability to deal with people, leading me to walk off the job, or shoot my mouth off before getting fired. Ultimately the need for resolve is paramount; it's a way to regain the control lost in a chaotic household where everything was out of control and nothing felt safe. Until then, I will continue to obsess over the situation. It doesn't just stop.

Children Need Safety and Structure to Thrive

I want to go back to my difficulty with mathematics and numbers, because there's an irony worth mentioning. Mathematics and numbers were easy for my dad; he'd often mention his talent for solving problems in his head. I thought, *Wow! That's really cool, Dad!* Sadly, he didn't have the patience to teach his children. The one time he came into my room to offer help with math was when I was in junior high. As soon as he discovered I didn't know my multiplication tables, he threw his hands up, exclaiming, "I can't help you. You don't even know your goddamn multiplication tables!!" and stomped out. He never offered again, and I never asked.

Pondering that thought, I felt so much anger toward my father for not helping me but criticizing me, for not participating in my life but expecting, expecting, always f… king expecting that I should somehow evolve into someone capable, competent, accomplished—someone more like himself! After all, I was his daughter. I probably wondered at that moment how that was supposed to happen, through f…king osmosis?!

Regarding homework, you must remember there was no accountability at home. Mom, no doubt, had been obsessing over Dad cheating on her and had the whole day for that idea to pick up momentum. Additionally, Mom had been tapping the keg for hours, primed for a verbal assault on him the instant he walked through the front door.

By the time I got home from school, my single objective was to escape unnoticed and unscathed into the hills behind our home on my motorcycle where another world existed: my refuge, where I was readily embraced by silence and beauty and calm. Once my home was out of sight, I could breathe and be a kid and ride with the boys, almost all of them my brother's friends, who also made those hills their playground. Most of the time I rode alone. I spent a lot of hours by myself.

Homework did not get done. Unfortunately, this was always followed by the dread of being called on by a teacher and the embarrassment at being unprepared. Thinking about it now, I was doing the best I could just to survive. Anything else didn't seem too important.

Depression came next, meaning I recognized depression for the first time in a big way at the end of a seven-year relationship. Depression picked up speed and spiraled down to a dark place of hopeless and despair. I didn't go mental over the loss of my relationship. The break-up was the straw that broke the camel's back and reinforced in a huge way the feelings I'd had all my life. I was intrinsically flawed and incapable of loving another person.

See You on the Dark Side of the Moon...

The severe depression and anxiety that followed led to two suicide attempts. I'm pretty sure I was out to destroy myself with many years of alcohol abuse and the accompanying behavior with its consequences. Three DUIs, three drunk in public, and a handful of other charges, five months in jail, two vehicles impounded and lost, homelessness in four counties for six months or more, and the list goes on. You could say I was bent on self-destruction, and you'd be right.

Depression Has Always Been a Part of My Life, Tugging Ruthlessly and Relentlessly on Me With One Goal in Mind: Annihilation!

Probably confused with the learning disability and never treated is attention deficit disorder (ADD). Except for the learning disability, depression and anxiety, other mental illnesses have never been diagnosed and treated correctly, so as to be non-issues in my life. I discovered attention deficit disorder while experimenting with cannabis. I was working outside, tending to my vegetable garden, when I recognized that it slowed my racing brain substantially, allowing me to recognize for the first time in sixty years how this played out in my life.

It's like multitasking. Beginning with one task, I may need a tool and go after it, and with a tool in hand, something else catches my eye. The transition from one task to the next is smooth. Things may not get completed on the first attempt because I'm easily distracted by something else that needs my attention, and on and on. I can have five or six unfinished tasks going at one time. Ultimately, things get done with a lot of zigs and zags but done perfectly, because like her father, Johanna's a perfectionist.

Something I've known all my life but never understood is why I don't read the instructions to put together things and don't follow directions well. That's easy. I have no patience and frustrate easily, traits I witnessed in my father while watching him at work. Maybe it's a comprehension issue. I do know that learning becomes easier when I can visualize it, hear it, and put my hands on it. As difficult as classes in anatomy and physiology were for me, I excelled in them because the subject matter held my interest, awe, and fascination. It was applicable to my work as a massage therapist.

If I think my way of doing something works better, I'm going to do it my way! This might tie in with ADD, and when coupled with the compulsion to do things perfectly and (inadvertently) against the stated wishes of my employer, you can see the potential for problems. Please understand that my decision is not a deliberate affront to my employer, and it is not me doing whatever the hell I want.

In an earlier conversation, my employer mentions wanting a particular thing done. It could have been two weeks or a day or an hour earlier. However, on this day with a backlog of projects and stressed about money, she changes her mind. I thought, *it'll take me two minutes to do that,* and I do it. When my employer discovers I did this, she blows a fuse and shouts at me for deliberately ignoring her directives and doing what I wanted. I thought, *Well, there's no argument there. I'm not seeing a problem. She's just a control freak.*

You see, *I've made a career out of anticipating the needs of others and meeting those needs.* It's in my DNA. It's how my brain is wired. It's what I've done all my life to earn my keep, and of course, it's done perfectly!

Post-traumatic stress disorder (PTSD) caused devastation and a whole lot of wreckage for me. One symptom of PSTD is I startle ridiculously easily, abruptly, and with great exaggeration by anything that takes me by surprise: loud sounds like car horns, sirens, something crashing and breaking, or any kind of unexpected BAM! BOOM! BANG! Oh my, the scary, crazy, volatile scene that occurred one time while stopped at a red light waiting to turn right. The sign above the light read No Right Turn on Red. Someone behind me laid on their horn—KABOOM! My adrenaline went through the roof as I slammed to a stop and slammed open my car door with every intention of dragging that person through their window and pummeling them into the pavement. Once I made eye contact and saw the look of horror in this poor girl's eyes, the size of saucers, I realized the raging lunatic I was being. Strangely, it didn't occur to me to question my behavior or think it odd. It was how I'd always been.

I live in an area with a lot of twisty canyon roads. I was hot-dogging down this steep canyon road through a sweeping turn at about 60 mph. Suddenly, I felt and heard this loud scraping sound from the foot peg on my left, dragging on the pavement. This was a new bike lowered from the factory to accommodate my five-foot-two frame, but I wasn't expecting that to happen! I was still in the turn when I startled, straightened my bike upright, and went off the road into a rain gutter on the right side of the road that was filled with rocks and debris. Being the professional rider that I am, ha ha, I was able to wrestle with the bike and keep it upright. I was so upset that I didn't ride for a long time afterward and put my bike up for sale. If I had been on the other side of the road, the sheer drop-off would have taken me out. Very scary!

Another way PTSD shows its face is through anger—"flipping the switch" kind of anger—and BAM! Explosive and scary, I'm told. That gets triggered when I'm personally affronted and feel threatened. I recall many times when I put myself in harm's way with people twice my size. It's like morphing into this super female action figure. I think my brain disengages, and my mouth switches to assault mode, running WFO (wide fucking open) until the person backs down in disbelief. It's a bad day for the person who gets in my face and causes me grief. (My life has been difficult enough without other people making it more difficult!!) The interesting thing is I'm not a fighter. I've never been in a fight, at least not physically. It's my mouth that goes off and scares the hell out of people, causing them to turn on their heel and flee from the crazy person. I can become like a woman possessed with unimaginable anger that I use like a weapon to slay my perceived enemies. I hope to find the answer as to where this anger comes from, who it was directed at initially, and why.

This leads to a significantly worse and dominating issue: obsessive-compulsive disorder (OCD) with a perfectionistic bent. When OCD is running the show, things only go from bad to worse, running riot in the workplace when I focus more on the task and less on the customer. This might give you a sense of the trouble this causes in customer service-related jobs.

I've always worked so hard with a sense of urgency and intensity, so meticulously and with such care and detail, *followed by angry outbursts when my efforts go unnoticed or when I feel unappreciated.* The greatest problem becomes one of *needing to be rewarded and the consequences when that reward is not forthcoming.* Like food, air, or water, this need is insatiable. As the song goes,

> *"I've been lookin' for love in all the wrong places,*
> *lookin' for love in too many faces..."*
>
> —*"Lookin' for Love" Pattie Ryan,*
> *Wanda Mallette, and Bob Morrison*

I want to mention that the object of my obsession could be one negative word spoken yesterday or weeks earlier. It gets stuck on a merry-go-round in my head and stays there until it is resolved.

The Lunatic Is in My Mind

Being witness to repeated violence in our home between our parents, the only caregivers we knew whose job it was to love and protect and didn't, the trauma is complex, devastating, and so far, irreversible.

I'm quoting my friend, Mike Johns, whose profound statement sums it up perfectly: "Such experiences have turned normal, healthy kids into walking pain machines of death, destruction, and scorched earth."

My battles with mental illness have been epic, tormenting me and undermining my relationships, friendships, and employment for over forty years. It's been only in the last couple of years that I've begun to understand any of this and recognize how these untreated issues have wrecked my life. It's been a shocking and devastating reality!

CHAPTER 6

A Child Pretender Is Born

At an early age, I became "Little Miss Perfect" by meticulously cleaning and caring for the house and yard for my parents so that they would acknowledge me, see my hard work, and notice the beautiful job I did. I needed them to see me, praise me, and validate me. They did not do any of these things; lots and lots of anger resulted. I think I was doing those things to help keep the peace at home. It became a serious game of survival of the fittest, and I happened to figure out how to play the game better than my siblings. Making matters worse, I was my mom's favorite. This created a whole lot of jealousy, resentment, and antagonism from my siblings but competition between my brother, Don, and me.

Once I spent time cleaning the house and making dinner for my family, thinking it would be a nice thing for my parents to come home to. Don came into the kitchen where I was setting the kitchen counter, and he started to mess up one of the place settings I was arranging. I grabbed the placemat from him and, in doing so, launched a butter knife through the air and into a large sliding glass door, which broke into a thousand pieces. I think my hard work did not get noticed that night. Don was always undermining my efforts like that.

Like my dad and his sister, whatever Don could do, I wanted to do as well, but he'd have no part in teaching me. Sadly, the wedge this put between my siblings and me continued throughout our adult lives and ended only with my brother's passing. It will be the same with my sister, Dana, as we have been estranged a number of years with no hope for reconciliation in sight. Incredibly sad, I know, but not for a lack of trying on my part.

To get to the core of this, I have to tell you more about my father. He was a critical and impatient man, self-centered, not demonstrative, and a perfectionist. It's not that he withheld love; he didn't know how to show it, because he was never shown love by his parents. I associated the absence of love by my father to mean I was not lovable or deserving of love.

Absent the good stuff—love without conditions, praise, validation, acceptance, support, encouragement, acknowledgment, and patience—the negative stuff got internalized and the concrete set.

A big part of the negative stuff for me was my father's impatience and criticism. In the absence of love and patience, to be criticized was to be judged and found lacking and a fate worse than death for this little perfectionist, propelling me to work harder. I came to believe that if I just worked hard enough, my parents would love me or maybe I'd get something close. That "something close" never came. When I am reminded of this, it makes me incredibly sad for that little girl who, at sixty-one, is still working hard to be loved.

I was my daddy's little girl in more ways than one, meaning I inherited his genes and his traits, and the smarts and potential that he and the women on his side of the family possessed. You can't imagine what it's like to recognize the potential in yourself and never be able to actualize it. It's like the proverbial carrot on a stick: in sight but always out of reach. It's cruel and painful. You become disillusioned and angry with life and God. No matter how hard you work, the American Dream is out of reach for you. Love, happiness, and success…out of reach. The alcohol abuse began.

CHAPTER 7

A Writer I Am Not

I am not a writer, and as someone who has great difficulty expressing thoughts and emotions, it's important to feel understood. I've spent much of my life feeling misunderstood. This, in part, I've discovered, has to do with self-sabotage. I often have trouble communicating my thoughts in their entirety. I know what I want to say, but as I move my mouth and the words come out, what I say is incomplete. There's a disconnect. Poof, gone! I lose my train of thought in the middle of the thought.

Another reason for not writing has to do with being an obsessive-compulsive bent on perfectionism. Oh my God!! I was such a freak about wanting my writing to look exactly right. If it didn't, I'd write again and again and again until it did or I ran out of paper or cards and trash my aborted efforts, resulting in cards and letters not being sent. That is so bizarre to me! Thank God for word processors! As I said, I'm not a writer, which makes writing this story an absolute labor of love to myself and maybe to others as well. I never had the patience, energy, or focus to stick with it. It is labor intensive. Mostly, it has been cathartic but not what I intended when I started out.

CHAPTER 8

A Journey of Insight and Awareness

———————◆———————

Regarding the anger I spoke of in Chapter 3, in addition to being a powerful, negative emotion, it can be different levels of scary for different people. I'd never given this any consideration, but because of a recent incident where I directed anger toward a dear friend, I was stopped in my tracks and forced to look at the way I learned to respond and how it continues to tear down my life and the relationships I desire.

You say, Well, that's a no brainer, stop the behavior! I'll reply that it's not something I *ever* felt I could control, or maybe subconsciously, I never wanted to let go of it. This Super Anger Avenger must have protected me as a child in a significant way, but as an adult, it has controlled me and enslaved me to a lifetime of loss and heartache.

This begs the question: How did using anger as a child serve me? *Was it the only weapon available to a small child that might stop Daddy from killing Mommy?* Coupled with launching a litany of expletives learned like a second language at home, did it make me feel less helpless or threatened? Was anger the only voice I had when I felt threatened or helpless? I don't know. I remember the first time I heard a parent tell their angry child "Calm down, Joey" and "Use your words." A smile came to my face, and I thought, *What a concept. Isn't that brilliant!*

Revisiting this anger, I mentioned in Chapter 3 a morphing and flipping the switch kind of anger, reserved for the dumb-ass who mistakenly gets in my face for the sole purpose of causing me grief. It's probably happened a dozen times.

The angry outbursts, volatile reactions, and limited ability to deal with people anger is what you might witness when my employment is terminated or as I am walking off another job, mouthing expletives for being unjustly criticized or blamed or talked down to or...well, there is a list of offenses that trigger this kind of angry reaction.

I find myself trying to dissuade you of the impression that I'm this raging whack-job on the loose, exacting revenge at the first opportunity on a world I've never felt a part of, for accidentally being bumped into, for someone crossing their eyes at me, or...whatever! Well, I can't exactly say the latter is entirely untrue.

CHAPTER 9

What You See Is Not Necessarily What You Get!

T he thoughts and emotions made transparent in Chapter 3 are an accumulation of experiences over the years and nothing you'd discern by looking at me. What you *would* discern is someone highly competent and capable, intensely hard working, responsible and resourceful, meticulous, thorough, and *focused to the point of not always smiling or acknowledging others.*

I worked hard to create and maintain this persona. Thinking about it now, I can see how this image has made me unapproachable, adding to a life already imprisoned by self-imposed isolation and unhappiness.

The Persona You See
Is the Persona I Want You to See

Do you recall the emergence of the "Child Pretender" in Chapter 3? This child, driven by the longing for love and validation, learned to perform, believing that if she worked hard enough, she'd get the love she craved. It was the agenda she approached each job with, but she was not cognizant of any agenda at the time.

The *focusing to the point of not acknowledging others* matter can go sideways when one of those others is a boss who gives directions not to do something and I do it. At the same time that I'm listening to directions, I'm more focused on what needs to be done, which might include the thing I was told *not* to do. Why would I do that, you ask? I don't know. However, I know that I'm especially observant, a skill I believed I learned as a child, anticipating the needs of my parents. As an adult, still eager to please, I've made a career of anticipating the needs of others. I look around, see what needs to be done, and do it. As a sufferer of OCD who is bent on perfection, I am *compelled* to be thorough and do things correctly and to completion. As a result, I often find myself working without pay to complete a job. Because I'm aware that I spend much more time than most people and not everyone wants to pay extra for that additional work—it's my problem. I wouldn't ask those people to pay. Oftentimes I get upset with myself for not being able to walk away from a job not completed. It makes me feel like such a freak. I don't see anyone else on this planet with this crazy behavior running their lives.

There's something else I've discovered about being a perfectionist. When I enter a room, for example, my attention is always drawn to what's wrong in the room first—the flaws—and I want to fix them. It's of great importance to me that things are exactly right, made prettier and better than before, and of course done perfectly. Otherwise, self-judgment will be harsh and swift.

CHAPTER 10

The Reward

—

I want to reiterate the importance of the *reward* I spoke of in Chapter 5 and the problems created when that reward is not forthcoming. The following story is the most vivid memory and example I have. It's been seared into my brain for the trauma it caused me as well as any nearby onlookers, I'm certain.

I helped open the Trader Joe's in San Luis Obispo in 1996. A kid my age who I'd been working circles around for six months got promoted. A promotion was the furthest thing from my mind. I was in college with a goal that did not include a management role at Trader Joe's, but the fact that he was promoted instead of me created instant animosity that I couldn't shake, setting my OCD-fueled brain on a merry-go-round of accelerated motion, left unattended to obsess over thoughts of being a better worker than he'd ever be, and what was wrong with me? Simultaneously, I'm tapping into the bottomless pit of emotional pain and memories of not feeling appreciated. This poor kid was not confident or competent and floundered terribly in his ability to manage the people under his charge, but worse, this included me.

Boundaries and Discipline Equal Safety and Love

I remember my mother chasing me into my bedroom, wielding a black rubber jump rope, hitting my bare backside as I scrambled over my bed to the other side far enough to avoid the sting of contact.

I was one pissed off, messed up, obstinate kid with a smart mouth, fluent in profanity and disrespect who *needed* to be managed for my own good. I needed someone to give a damn and discipline me, washing my mouth out with soap each time I thought using the f-word was a smart idea. An out-of-control kid constantly suffering from the results of poor decisions cries out for boundaries—they feel safer within the confines of rules and consequences, because they know what to expect, and I needed consistency, which to me equals love. I didn't get that kind of love, and man, did that screw me up!

Sadly, as a result of my parent's neglect, little by little, I think I lost respect for them. As someone who can attest, this never turns out good. When the dust settles, there will be no happy ending, only more confusion, anger, shame, and guilt. Similarly, when respect is lost for someone in authority over me, especially law enforcement, I can be a nightmare to manage.

I want to add that seeing my mom as a victim of my father's abuse deepened my disdain and intolerance for what I perceive as weakness in others and in myself. It disturbs me beyond measure to see anyone being harmed in any way at the hands of another. Being forced to watch violence in our home between my parents triggered massive anger and anxiety that overwhelms me with a sense of urgency, and I need to make it stop, or I have to get away. I've walked out of movies and won't hesitate to launch myself into the fray when I witness a verbal altercation between two people turn physical. What happens to me when a guy puts his hands on a woman in a menacing way is nothing short of crazy. I will shoot like an arrow to intervene and fearlessly go nose to nose with the perpetrator like a crazed madwoman.

Like a Wild Donkey Accustomed to the Wilderness, I Am Angry, Mistrusting, and Rebellious

I was destined to repeat this behavior. No surprise that I could not take orders from this kid at Trader Joe's. The fireworks began when he decided to use his newly acquired authority to suspend me for insubordination. We got into a public altercation as coworkers and customers looked on. He acted like an idiot, lacking the experience and confidence to know how to handle difficult situations, and I acted like a woman possessed. This was the "angry outburst, volatile reactions, and limited ability to deal with people" anger that I felt was justified as I thought about how hard I worked, doing everything asked of me and then some, working with such thought, care, and detail—things nobody else would even think of doing. How could my boss not see this and acknowledge me, praise me, and promote me??

The following day, I approached my boss and asked him why I wasn't promoted. Seeing my tears, he gently replied, "I'm sorry, Johanna. You ruffle feathers, and Mark doesn't."

I exclaimed, "But John, Mark's an idiot, and..."

Walking away, I was confounded at being fired.

CHAPTER 11

Mental Illness Changed the Trajectory of My Life

T his is one of many similar examples that have dominated my life and undermined my ability to keep a
job and support myself. As a result, I have lost nearly
everything I've come to own. I've never had a home. The
longest I've lived in one location is seven years, then four,
but most often around one to two years. The rest of the
time I've bounced around like a gypsy, oftentimes homeless, sleeping in my car and drinking myself unconscious
in an effort to escape my unbelievably insane and depress-
ing reality.

I never had kids for fear of perpetuating the dysfunc-
tion I grew up in. I couldn't take care of myself, so why
would I want to bring an innocent life into my nightmare?
I couldn't! Nor was I relationship material—normal, healthy,
loving behavior was not modeled in our home, and you
can't give what you don't have! Unfinished emotional gar-
bage continued to interfere with the life I wanted and was
a huge factor for never marrying.

You're probably thinking, *Jesus, get some therapy!!*
I have, and I am a testament to the quality of mental

health care available to the working-class poor in our country. It's substandard, inadequate at best, at addressing the pain and issues caused by childhood trauma. A limited number of thirty-minute visits per year doesn't begin to cover it.

CHAPTER 12

The Perfect Storm

In 2017, my troubles came to a head as a result of being fired or laid off from three jobs back-to back, two car accidents in one year, a suspended license, a hit-and-run charge added to my record that had just become clear, three years of probation, fines, fees, and forty hours of community service. There are a least three good stories in this paragraph that I won't go into right now.

The first accident had the potential to be a much greater catastrophe than it was. It occurred while backing up a steep, narrow incline with room for only one vehicle. It was raining. Impatient and annoyed, I backed up in haste, looking over my right shoulder, and veered off the left side of the road, sliding sideways to a stop on a steep embankment. Had my vehicle continued to slide and then roll, I probably wouldn't be sitting here writing this story. I learned how steep this embankment was when I opened the driver's door. I dropped straight down six or eight feet into loose, damp dirt, rocks, and tree limbs that stopped my car from continuing to roll.

The following day, I discovered the annoying irritation and rash on the exposed parts of my body that could only come from poison oak. Damn!

An hour earlier that day, I was fired from a job I loved without any explanation of my crime, based solely on the words of a kid who misinterpreted a gesture I made in frustration that was not intended for him. An intense altercation with my boss began the minute I was handed my paycheck and told I was fired. I left there upset and not thinking clearly. The slight buffer that usually came with taking my meds as prescribed was not present. I've come to understand this is of monumental importance, as just one day without them creates a subtle irritation that leads to negativity, depression, and anxiety. Three days without them seriously screws with the brain chemistry, and the effects, including slurred words, light headedness, and disorientation, are scary.

The second accident brought this subject to a head. It began the morning of April 4, 2017. I had a job interview, the first one since being fired. The house was full of people visiting: ten adults, six kids, and five dogs making a lot of commotion. I was on the computer getting directions and hurrying when I began to get irritated and anxious. I had to get out of the house.

I must have missed something in my direction taking because I got lost. The irritation and anxiety I brought with me tripled. I don't know about you, but I drive faster when I'm upset. Looking for my phone to call the employer, I realized I left it at home. Irritation turned to self-loathing and anger as I drove faster, looking for a business that might have a phone I could use. Spotting a twenty-four-hour Family Fitness, I come to a screeching stop in the parking lot and slammed open my car door. I ran to the glass doors, managing to calm myself enough to ask to use the phone. I made my call but was unable to keep the agitation out of my voice. There would be no interview that day or tomorrow.

Driving back home, I was crying, bordering on hysteria over my rotten stinking life.

My mom was in an alcohol-related car accident my senior year. I was fifteen and a half when she died at home a month later from a pulmonary aneurysm. I didn't cry when I was told. I didn't know what to feel.

Dad began frequenting the bars in search of a mother for us kids. Six months later, he brought home "Dottie, the Deceitful Gold Digger." I think children are much more intuitive than they get credit for. I never liked her from the start and for good reason as it turned out. On one occasion, we got into a doozy of a verbal altercation, and in her best French-Canadian-Indian voodoo voice, she told me she was putting a curse on me. The way my life has gone, I've often wondered.

I remembered I needed to stop by the pharmacy and refill a prescription, and I was not in a good frame of mind. I became extra annoyed, running back and forth from one pharmacy to the next because there was a screwup. On the second trip back to Walgreens, the clerk manning the counter caught my wrath for picking up the phone just as I approached instead of acknowledging me. I said some terrible things to him, slammed out of the store, knocked over a merchandising display, sprinted to my car, and sped off.

With my nervous system amped and far from thinking clearly, I was driving like an insane person, easily going 100 mph on a road designed for 35 mph. I blew through a stop sign around a vehicle stopped there and continued until I came to a stop. I tapped the bumper of the Toyota Tundra stopped at a red light in front of me. Backing up and pulling over to the side, I got out of my vehicle and jogged up to the window to apologize to the woman. I told her the damage to her bumper was minimal, but my car was toast. Her reply, as she was getting out of her truck, was "I'll be the judge of that!" With exactly the wrong tone and attitude, I thought, *Oh, no, this can only get worse.*

As she was taking pictures of the damage, I lost patience, turned on my heel, walked back to my vehicle, got in, and drove home. Within ten minutes, a black-and-white appeared at my house, as I knew it would. I made the mistake of blurting something about medication not working and not thinking clearly. That turned out to be a bad idea!

With a combination of stressors and emotional triggers, a nervous system gone berserk, ineffective medication or no medication to treat a combination of mental health issues *concurrently,* add vehicular recklessness to the mix, and I was out of control and headed into a big shit storm of new problems.

CHAPTER 13

You Can't Change What You Don't Understand

U sing cannabis in experimental amounts for a desired effect has played a significant role in gaining new insight that otherwise would be unavailable. Who knew vaping a little weed would be the key to unlocking doors, gifts of insight, and greater understanding behind them? Having an addictive personality, however, the challenge is not abusing it. I'm working on finding balance. In the meantime, I'm going to enjoy the hell out of it, because I like how I feel about myself. It lightens me up when my normal disposition is to take life way too seriously. I am more social and outgoing, initiating conversations I normally would not with people, with patience and interest. More than that, I enjoy the person I am when I lighten up. I laugh at myself, joke more, and can be stupid silly and not care what anyone thinks about this sixty-one-year-old, slightly odd but kindhearted and likable woman.

As I began taking inventory of my life, I started to see the pattern, recognizing with vivid clarity for the first time *ever* the reasons for the crazy and dramatic work-related episodes and repeated loss of jobs. I was devastated and bewildered. The fact that this was a true story was what made it so unbelievably bizarre to me.

After being fired from my last job, I started writing down everything that happened that day: my thoughts and feelings, triggers, and angry behavior, witnessing OCD and PTSD behavior intertwined throughout (the two most predominant culprits), tormenting me intermittently my entire life, leaving a wasteland of my life and a legacy to no one.

Why I Began This Story

Depression raced in with a vengeance to claim victory, and it lasted two months. As more truth and insight came, more depression and anxiety followed until I could not take anymore! I was so tired of fighting just to survive. Exhausted and defeated, I was unable to give any more effort to what seemed like one big, fat, cruel joke that I was the butt of. I was at my lowest; I was done with this nightmare called "My Life." I wanted to be dead. I was contemplating the possibility for a kinder, gentler future absent loss, sorrow, and suffering, and it wasn't something being offered as an option. I had been going through the motions of living life for a long, long while, and I wondered why I should. I couldn't think of one single reason!

Pondering this, I thought, *If I died today, not one soul, not one other human being on this planet, would know anything about what my life was really like.* That prospect was too sad and inconceivable to consider. I knew in that moment I wasn't going anywhere until I told this story. I was handed a purpose to live and began the journey of putting my story in writing.

Like a Leaf in the Wind, I Am Storm Tossed and Without Comfort

I could never understand where the loving God, whose son I fell in love with and whose teachings I tried to live my life by, was in the fiasco called my life. I felt abandoned by a sovereign God who promised never to leave or forsake me. Like my father, I felt abandoned by God. How do you put your trust and faith in someone like that? I couldn't.

After twelve years of longing for spiritual intimacy with the Living God, this too was out of reach. At some point, wanting to understand why this was so, I started on a personal quest, chasing after answers, beginning with reading every self-help book I could find. I went to conferences and workshops and listened to different teachings, all of which led me to the one concept that rang a bell. The "wounded child within" was calling the shots. As I became more aware, it did not take long to recognize that I had transferred my dad issues onto the loving God of the Universe who did not resemble that comparison at all, ever! My relationship with God had always been performance oriented, crazy neurotic, and fear based, making the truest, most pure love without conditions unattainable.

Another Reason for Writing This Story

Confirmation regarding writing my story came immediately from two additional sources. If you remember the theme of the 2019 Academy Awards, it was about the "Me Too" movement. I heard two things that nudged me to begin writing: *the empowerment that comes with "shouting your name" and "telling your story!"*

The third reason and incident that led to telling this story was learning I had been left out of the "40 Years of

Women's MX History and Celebration." As a champion, hero, legend, and pioneer, I was an important part of it. Instead of going after the persons involved in the deception (one in particular), I was encouraged to tell my story. Considering this idea, I thought, *Yeah, okay, I will tell a story, but it's not going to be what people might expect!*

Motorcycles Saved My Life Again

At some point in this mix, I received a phone call from a Vintage Motocross promoter, Dave Boydstun, who invited me out to his Vintage MX event in Arizona where I would be recognized as Legend, Pioneer and Champion of Women's Professional MX from the seventies. "By the way," he said, "I've got a 250 cc CZ for you to take a few laps around the track on." Mind you, I had not been on a dirt bike in forty years, and the last thing I wanted to do was break my neck or make a fool of myself. I asked if I was going to have some time to practice! Dave replied, "Yeah, you'll have a day before the event to practice." I thought, *One day?!* I panicked.

With six weeks to go before this event and a small goal for the first time in I don't know how many years, I upped my weight program a little, giving attention my back, core, and forearms. I vividly recall my forearms fatiguing quickest and what that felt like. Since I'd weight trained all my life, I was fit. I did not want to fall off my bike because my forearms seized up and I couldn't hang on to the handlebars. That would be lame and dangerous. A trip back through the old scrapbook to times of greatness influences your ego, and your faulty judgment leads you to believe that you can jump back on a dirt bike and ride like you used to after forty years. Even knowing I couldn't, I'd act like I could and likely get hurt.

The instant I set that goal, I was put in touch with the extraordinary young girl that I was back then: a self-taught, fiercely tenacious little athletic with heart and talent who lived to train and race motorcycles.

I was still struggling with alcohol but quit because it wasn't consistent with being an athlete then or now. I haven't wanted a drink since. To understand the magic of this, you'd have to know that I struggled with alcoholism on and off for about twenty years with little success—winning a battle here and there but ultimately always losing the war.

Dave Boydstun had no idea the timely impact that phone call had in changing the course of my life, lifting the preoccupation I had with wanting to be dead and awaking that part of me I hadn't recognized in a long time.

Around the same time, I was visiting my doctor who had seen me through my battles with booze and mental health—crisis after crisis in the aftermath of losing another job and wrecking my car. This was a significant accomplishment that baffled the medical team that came to my rescue in force: the doctor, therapist, and psychiatrist who saw me only as a screwed up, struggling, ineffectual adult.

We talked a little about being an athlete and having goals and how that was the spark that ignited the flame in me. Of course, the obvious solution was to get a motorcycle and get riding again. Ha, ha! That idea, along with each dream, wish, want, hope, and desire, has remained just that: a dream, wish, want, hope, and desire.

The final reason for writing this story is to have at my disposal information to reference as needed when I am questioned by the administrative judge handling my Social Security Disability case. I was on the final leg of a claim

I filed in June 2015. The court date to see the wizard was June 10, 2019.

A question like, "Ms. Stenersen, please tell the court why you claim your disabilities have made you unemployable?" I was told claims like mine are never easy to win, but I would win. I had to!

During deliberations before the judge made his decision, I was impatiently thinking how obvious it should be and wanted to say, "Just look at my work history, Your Honor. Is there any denying that I don't keep jobs long and can't support myself? Isn't that enough?" My lawyer stopped me at, "Just look at my work history," before I could go any further. She knew something I didn't, so I kept my mouth shut after that.

In case I didn't make it obvious, the little girl with great heart, tenacity, and spirit of a warrior, the one who endured unrelenting blows due to mental illness and a lifetime of defeat to bounce back time and again? She is the hero in this story.

CHAPTER 14

God?

his is another story I wanted to tell because of the timing and content. I find it exciting when God shows up as anything becomes possible.

A huge born-again Christian movement started in the sixties (I believe). These radical believers began a church in a tent in the Orange County town of Costa Mesa in California. It became the mothership to hundreds of smaller offshoot churches known as Calvary Chapel.

I must have had a sizable target on my back, because in 1978, Christians were everywhere, coming out of the woodwork, intent on telling me about Jesus. It was textbook discipleship, and I acquiesced. I loved the teachings of Jesus and fell in love with the God who promised me unconditional love and acceptance. Like a starving child, I was hungry and receptive.

I walked away from God and His church when the behavior of God's people didn't line up with God's teaching. I needed acceptance without judgment and consistency, all of which stopped. After twelve years, I left, angry and disillusioned.

Several weeks prior to writing chapter 14, I kept hitting roadblocks, one after another, and I was frustrated. I needed to get outside, get some exercise, and breathe some fresh air. I went to a trail I knew of. Instead of going left on the trail I knew, I went right on a new trail, moving carefully down a steep decline of clay and loose granite rock. I'd had shoulder surgery recently and was on pain meds with my arm in a sling. I encouraged myself out loud that I could do this without falling on my ass and sliding to the bottom (reminding myself that my innate abilities as an athlete should make this a breeze). Managing this, I continued along a narrow hiking trail enclosed by glistening, green grass, the new growth that comes with the first winter rains. *Awwww, this is nice,* I thought.

As I hiked farther in, I began thinking about mountain lions. Seeing the sign on the way in probably had something to do with that. There had been sightings and domestic animals missing, their bones and fur found nearby. A woman was killed by a mountain lion close to where I was.

Finding a sunny spot, I stopped on the trail to stretch and look for a club of some sort. Looking around, I begin to feel nervous, thinking, *this is winter. Mountain lions don't hibernate, and they're probably hungry this time of year, and...* I began talking out loud, up toward the cosmos to a God I was not certain listened. "I'm good if being eaten by a lion is how I am to leave this planet," adding, "Please make it quick," depicted by snapping my fingers. At the same time, I envisioned a huge, outstretched, dark blur of a figure launched in my direction from a nearby oak and then BAM! SNAP! DONE! With a sigh of relief, I thought, *Now that's mercy!* I thought about where I'd end up. Uh-oh. I wasn't entirely sure.

I went farther down the trail, out of the shaded area and into the sunlight. I wanted to feel the warmth of the sun on my face; looking up, I found myself praying for my salvation. Seconds of silence passed as I contemplated the meaning behind my words. "Out of love for *me*, Jesus, you had to die." *Your blood washes over me, and I am cleansed.* My knees weakened a little, but I was comforted by the knowledge that I was righteous in the eyes of Holy God. I was humbled.

Infused with new certainty, I continued hiking all of fifteen feet before stopping abruptly, looking up, and grasping my head in my hands. I exclaimed incredulously, "Jesus Christ, my f...king life! God? Why?" Blistering fast images of my life came into my mind's eye—my sufferings, mental illness, sin, sadness, isolation and loss, loss, loss—and again I asked, *Why?* "Did you bring me through forty f...king years of misery and...and wilderness for no reason except to die?"

Hmmm, I thought. *I've heard this story before.* When it came to me, I said out loud, "Oh no, no, no...please don't tell me that the last forty years has been my wilderness experience or that you allowed it to teach me something I've insisted on learning the hard way."

Nope, not going there! It would screw with my head if I didn't keep mental illness and sin separate. I did not believe that sinful behavior as a result of mental illness caused by an untreated chemical imbalance in the brain could be condemned. Thus, the reason for the insanity plea.

I've experienced far too much sorrow and suffering, too many unmet needs and unanswered prayers to believe God genuinely cares about me, thus, reducing God to more of a concept than a personal God. Subsequently, I don't put a lot of time or energy into prayer anymore. My reasoning has been, "If I don't ask, I won't be disappointed or angry." I know this parallels the way I viewed my dad, including my smart mouth and flagrant display of irreverence toward the God of the Universe, but it is where things stand right now. It's a love-hate relationship that I have with Holy God, same as my father, and I haven't been successful at untangling the two. It sounds absurd, doesn't it? Well, my life has been absurd!

CHAPTER 15

Eight Months Later

T his next part of this story is a running commentary and compilation of past and current events, replete with poor choices, bad behavior, and ugly truths. You'll see specific emotional triggers in action and reactions that the average person would deem intense, bizarre, and scary, but for me, it's my norm and has been for decades.

After posting Part 4 of my story on Facebook, what was perplexing about the replies I received from friends and family was that not one person said, "Johanna, I'm sorry for what you went through," or asked how I was doing, or asked if they could help in some way. Some were encouraging that I continue to write, chanting, "Book! Book! Book!" I am sure some didn't know how to respond and therefore did not. Many didn't read my story at all. I learned it is much too long of a read for the attention of span of your average Facebook user on the fly. Plus, it is a tough story to read and even tougher to imagine when the writer is someone you know in real life and not a character in a novel, or have we become too indifferent and jaded toward the painful plights of others?

Lastly, I was aware that Facebook was not the best platform to launch my story that was so transparent, personal, and raw. As I said, I needed somebody to know what my life has been like because of mental health issues—the stories have been unreal, and *my life a tragic, sad story of survival, heartache, and suffering.* It was the only platform available to me, consisting mostly of my seventies motocross community and high school classmates, most of whom were a year ahead of me and in my brother's class. I didn't know any of them well, including those who were my own classmates. Back then, I was too socially awkward and insecure to make friends. Of course, to conceal my shame, I transformed without haste into my cool, aloof, motorcycle chick persona who was the little sister of her cool and popular older brother, Don.

CHAPTER 16

Now What?

From the outset of attempting to write Part 5, I struggled with terrible depression. I had zero motivation to continue writing. After all, I did achieve my goal to get the real story of my life outside of myself and into the Universe, to leave a small thread behind supporting the truth of my existence.

I was feeling off kilter and wondering, *Now what?* Turning my attention upward and speaking out loud, I asked, "What about you showing up on the trail, Jesus?" I was hoping to turn a corner with my story to something more positive and hopeful with possibilities for a life worth getting excited about. Otherwise, there was no story to tell. End of story!

Perhaps there's some grand (or not so grand job) for me to do while I'm still here that necessitates having and sharing these miserably debilitating and humiliating mental health experiences, but no, nada, nothing!

Having no patience, I easily slip backward and into a downward spiral emotionally, accompanied by a grasping attitude and attempt at controlling my life and my future. I say, "As far as I'm concerned, the only next for me needs to include winning my SSD case and getting a monthly income with consistency for the first time, which will barely scratch the surface of my financial needs."

To sustain me and have a life other than the one I've known, the life I want, I need a substantial influx of money, promised to me by my father and declared in his trust. There are big issues and a lot riding on the outcome being in my favor, because like my father, I've equated God's love for me with the outcome. Without it, I'll be forced to continue down the same path as before, which is just existing. I won't do that!

I've been in a standoff with God over this for a while now. (I know how lame this sounds.) I've never been able to trust God when it matters. I've asked God for proof of his love for me. Then I'll trust. You'll better understand what's at issue here in a later chapter.

Holy God, I need your love to be real and tangible, not wishful or magical thinking from naive beliefs in the promises of Jesus. Universe, please, I could use a break, a little divine favor to make up for my parent's lack. I need to believe I will be taken care of and that the enemy won't win at destroying my life. Dear God, I need to know there's hope for healing and transformation and that I'll find it. It's the only thing that will suffice.

This, among other things, has required waiting, waiting, and more waiting beyond what I think I am capable of enduring. I'm not familiar with this kind of mental anguish. With my need for money being so great, the pain I feel from having to keep waiting has been excruciating!

CHAPTER 17

Not Feeling the Love

As you'll see, I have huge issues surrounding my father and his money, mainly because he had plenty yet wouldn't part with any of it to help one of his children advance in life. A reoccurring question that caused me many years of deep heartbreak and anguish when it came to mind was this: "What parent wouldn't want to give their child every opportunity to succeed if they had the means?" My dad always had the means but apparently was not interested in helping me succeed. *That did not stop him from expecting me to succeed.* Trying and failing, then working harder and still being unable to succeed made me angrier and angrier, more resentful of my father, and deeply loathing of myself.

If you'll recall, I told you that my father was a good provider and that it was his way of showing his love for us. It's what I believed until we turned eighteen, and that's when his responsibilities ended. All attempts my father made to cut the cord failed miserably, and I am certain he felt disappointed and bewildered by my lack of success. After all, I was my father's daughter.

I think you can understand why I made the leap, concluding that he didn't love me. Reinforcing this were the many attempts I made when asking for help with college that were shot down with statements like "I had a college fund for you kids, but your mother spent all of it on new furniture." Unspoken but clearly understood was that it wasn't of much importance to him. I interpreted this to mean I wasn't of much importance to him. Here's a favorite; he'd say, "If I help you, then I'll have to help all the rest of you," meaning my two siblings who had no interest in going to college and the two new stepsisters from his second marriage to "Dottie, the Deceitful, Gold-Digging Witch." Sadly, and ironically, it was discovered that Dottie had been helping herself as she pleased to my father's money without his knowledge to do just that: help put one of her daughters through Cal Poly, San Luis Obispo. I know this because I ran into the daughter, Maryanne, one day as I was walking toward a popular brew and food place where she was leaving following her shift. When I asked how she was able to fund college when working part-time, she replied, "Oh, Mom sends me money."

Dottie didn't work. She didn't have to. She got whatever she wanted and pilfered the rest from my father's bank accounts that she had access to whenever she felt like it. She had her sights set on his money from the start. As I stated in an earlier chapter, Dad frequented the bars in search of a mother for us kids when my mom died in 1972. Advertising his wealth and success proved to be a bad idea. What kind of women do you suppose that'll attract? It'll attract the morally skanky, gold-digging types who frequent bars exactly for that purpose. Duh!

It was a confusing time for all of us. Dad brought home Dottie and her two daughters, both of whom were much more adept at communicating their wants and needs to my father than any of us were. The attention Dad showed Dottie's girls, and which he was unable to show us, triggered a huge revolt in the heart of this hurting little girl.

I ran away from home shortly after that to live with my best friend, Sue Fish, her sister, (Diane), Mom (Angela), and stepdad (Bob) in Monterey Park, California. They were a kind and loving family. I'd never had a friend like that before, and it was fun as hell to run around together doing whatever!

Had we been living together as just friends instead of "friends plus fierce rivals," things would not have been so tough on me. I lived among my competitor's greatest fans and supporters—her family and friends. Living in enemy territory wore on me. It was difficult to gain a psychological advantage over your opponent when you were in that kind of situation, and it necessitated me moving out.

I wanted to ask for help with the courses I struggled with most because of my disabilities by getting a tutor. It wasn't a need I was able to articulate or convey to my father, so I didn't. My father didn't go to college, and therefore, the idea of it was not a priority in his sphere of experience. It was never spoken of.

He recognized my talent for racing motorcycles but could not understand why I repeatedly failed at the rest of my life. It wasn't until late in his life that he told me he was proud of me for my racing achievements. In addition, he kept the trophy I got for winning the District 37 #1 plate in Women's Expert Motocross in his office. Seeing it there one day, I made the comment that I was surprised to see he kept it. His reply was that "he kept it for good luck." I felt nothing. My heart was calloused with scar tissue from being broken and neglected for too many years.

As mentioned, I did not feel prepared to face life, reinforced by the repeated challenges and defeats related to my mental health issues. Having such a terrible fear of failure, I was constantly dropping college classes if I thought I might fail, and if I didn't think I could try something new and do it well, I wouldn't try at all. This is clearly the perfectionist in action.

I don't ever recall a parent offering comfort or encouragement when I felt afraid and overcome with self-doubt or in my OCD, spinning a tale in my head at Mach speed. Had I been comforted by a loving parent and told in a soothing tone "I've got you, it's going to be okay" or "It's okay, you can do this" or "I'm with you, let's do this together," it would have gone a long way in changing the tides and kept this little girl from being sucked under by her mental and emotional riptide.

I recall a time around 1977 when I was sitting on the starting line at the Women's Nationals at Rawhide Motorcycle Park. Back in those days, we rode two grand prix on Saturday, two hours each, on a 125 cc and then a 250 cc. On Sunday, we rode four motos, 125 and 250 cc classes, thirty or forty-five minutes each.

One day, we were revving our bikes in anticipation of the gate dropping when the muscles in my neck and shoulder on the right side seized up, making it too painful to turn my head when the gate dropped.

Two hours was a long time for this little girl with attention deficit to stay focused without difficulty. I was held up on a narrow part of the track by slower riders, and I watched with a sinking heart as Sue pulled farther away. I was running a distant second behind her and close to the end of the race when I attempted to pass a slower rider in an easy, left-hand turn with a low berm. I don't recall much of anything about the rest of the track accept the start and that corner as I went high over the top of the berm and into a dense thicket on the other side and became trapped. I was exhausted and quickly went from panic to frantic as I tried to pull my bike free from the brush and couldn't. The race ended shortly after that, and I ended up finishing seventh.

In hindsight, that was one of the rare times I experienced a traumatic event that impacted me like that, convincing me that I could face a similar fate if I went back out and raced the final event that day.

When I got into the pits, still rattled, I declined to go back out. With the exception of my dad, I don't recall anyone else being around when I announced I wasn't going back out that day. The reason I gave was that I wanted to save myself for the four motocross events the following day. Without comfort, support, or a challenge, I disqualified myself and sabotaged any chances of becoming the Overall Grand National Champion, but I wasn't paying attention to that or seeing the big picture. I was allowing fear to make my decisions for me.

As an observation, I didn't experience the effects of mental illness in my youth to the extent that I have as an adult. I think the amount of exercise and training I was doing at the time played a role by generating enough serotonin, endorphins, and dopamine (the body's natural crack) to tone down the effects of some mental illnesses. My brain was missing the serotonin, which, in my case, keeps depression and anxiety at bay. My body was manufacturing serotonin but unable to get where it needed to go to be of any benefit.

As it turned out, I won three of the four motos, sliding out in the first moto as the track had just been watered. I don't remember where I placed, but at the end of the day, I missed the title by one point. I wasn't aware Sue had fallen a couple times as well. I honestly believe I was as fast as her. The biggest difference between us was luck and support. Sue had a better network of support from family and her sponsor, Crown Cycle, which maintained her bikes better than I did mine. If the tables were turned and Sue was in my position, there would be no way her father would let her quit like I did without serious repercussions. Sue's dad, Ed Fish, could be a mean son of a bitch and a bully, especially when he drank. Not that I would want that type of support, but you get the idea, right?

In the early days, it seemed to me that oftentimes Sue rode beyond her means, fearful of her father's wrath if she didn't win. Evidence of this, I believe, lay in the ridiculous number of broken bones sustained during her racing career. Sue had no competition there.

Without question, Sue's biggest support came from her mom, Angela. Their relationship seemed to be fun loving, playful, and emotionally supportive. Her lovely sister, Diane, taught her about fashion and makeup. They were close as sisters, and it was a loving family.

Looking back, it's also my belief that having support made the difference between being the Overall Champion and being Number Two, and missing the Overall Title by one point. I left racing at the tail end of 1977 primarily because of the lack of support. Also, there didn't seem to be a future in Professional Women's MX. The unsubstantial purses being offered to women at the time didn't make continuing worthwhile. There were not enough fast, talented women racers to draw the spectators or sponsors until the 1980s.

Things Learned

I typically think in black and white, all or nothing, and I am impulsive—the predominant attributes of being a perfectionist. As I've discovered, things are rarely that way in reality. Because I seem intent on focusing on the negative, I see the negative side of things before seeing the positive. I didn't see a future for Women's Motocross. Apparently, there was a future for Women's Motocross, but I didn't see it and moved on without a backward glance.

With motocross being a predominantly male sport, some women were at the mercy of the men in their lives for financial support and to maintain their bikes unless they were exceptionally mechanically inclined and worked on their own bikes. A boyfriend might walk out of a female racer's life because of a breakup or if she was unwilling to "put out" as a condition of her sponsor's continued involvement. A lot of women were reliant on those male relationships to be able to continue racing.

CHAPTER 18

The Beginning of the End

On July 15, 2018, I was evicted from the place where I had lived for four years as unresolved emotional issues and anger from past hurtful scenarios played out unabated in the present, scaring my friend/landlord to death, and ruining our relationship. I've been sleeping in my car and destitute since then. It's January 2021.

It's a significant story on my timeline in terms of the persons involved.

I was able to recognize some old emotions and behaviors that got triggered as a result of unresolved pain. There was excellent potential for a tremendous learning and growth experience for both of us; regretfully, it did not go that way. Like all the others, my dear friend became a casualty of my continued internal war.

I met Helga—a tall German woman who was intelligent, charming, kind, and caring—when I was the marina host at Lake Clementine where she kept her boat from May to October 2012. At the completion of the season, she invited me to stay on her property in Auburn with my Dodge Road Trek motorhome, return for a second season to the lake, and then go back to Helga's home. I never left.

For about four years, Helga recognized my talent for hard work as well as my difficulties keeping a job. She could not understand my personal struggles with depression and fear and the shame that paralyzed me each time I got fired. I couldn't explain how OCD, PTSD, perfectionism, and angry episodes consistently undermined my life and ability to keep a job.

Helga bent over backward for me and was generous with her time, energy, and money in trying to help me. She wanted to see me succeed. She made every effort to include me in social and family events and all other special occasions. In a lot of ways, she treated me like a daughter, although she'd be the first to tell you she had two daughters and did not need another. She told me she "did not want the additional worry or responsibility." She was a worrier like no other. If she loved or cared for someone, she did so deeply. That statement came after witnessing and not understanding the repeated problems in my life, created by mental health issues or my behavior.

Initiated by me, ours was a tacit arrangement. It was an ideal arrangement for me and a safe place to be as OCD and perfect as my heart desired without negative repercussions. Helga was so easy going and appreciative of everything I did for her that doing anything was a pleasure.

She trusted me with the run of her home, yard, and fenced-in garden area, which I turned into a beautiful space to grow fruit and vegetables exactly how I wanted. The only rule was that I should grow organic, and I couldn't be happier. Unbeknown to me, this lovely garden and home would become my refuge and classroom, the small neighborhood on Bridgeview Drive my community and a place I hoped to stay.

In the end, Helga realized she couldn't fix me and stopped trying. I'm sure she was disappointed and bewildered over that. Experiencing my anger frightened the hell out of her, and she told me she wouldn't live with it. She had to push, drag, and shove me out of my safe and comfortable little nest and the only place I'd ever lived for four and a half years. It was only in the last year that it felt like a home and I began taking things out of boxes and putting them in drawers.

Two summers previous, a friend of Helga, Dana, asked me if I was interested in some work, and I said sure. I knew he was a jackass and pulled shady deals. Helga herself had been a victim of one of his unsavory business deals, and he owed her a lot of money that he never intended to repay. I didn't understand why she continued to befriend someone like that. She said, "Dana has his usefulness to me." I saw a side of Helga that made compromises to serve her purposes even as Dana showed his true colors as a liar, cheat, and a thief. I was dumbfounded by this.

I did hard physical work for this guy. I had to nag him to get paid at the end of each work week until he decided not to pay me at all. Well, I guess my revenge trigger got pushed, and one early morning, I rode my motorcycle out to the job site with criminal intentions in mind. After searching for a way to disable the heavy equipment he left at the site, I noticed that he left the keys in the ignitions of both pieces of equipment, so I took the keys and was on my bike, ready to leave, when Dana drove up. With a knowing look on his face, he moved quickly to his equipment to discover what he feared had happened. I started my bike and sped off. All the jerk had to do was pay me the money he owed me, and I would give him back his keys. He would not.

Things went on its ass when retelling this story to Helga. If the expression on her face didn't communicate horror and dismay, her words did as she told me my behavior was not normal. What I heard was "you are not normal." I replied, "It was normal in my neighborhood," meaning that because I was not able to rely on parents for help, I had to take situations into my own hands or allow others to take advantage of me and get away with it.

She replied, "Well, it's not normal in this neighborhood."

Things went from bad to worse as I began accusing her of siding with Dana, telling her, "You condemn my behavior, but you condone his?"

I think by this time my voice had raised an octave. I felt betrayed by my friend. The words resonating deep within the recesses of my mind—"You believe him and not me" and "why are you taking his side and punishing me?"—felt like something I'd say to my mom regarding my brother.

This was our first argument in four years, but it was the beginning of the end of my stay in Helga's home. She came down to my room later and told me that she'd never been yelled at like that before. I suspect that was a trigger for her, as she had expressly stated not wanting anger or drama in her home.

I understood, but I could not keep it from happening again when Helga took a tenant in to rent the two-bedroom apartment next door with the nicest living room, the nicest big-screen TV, and the nicest shower for a steal: $500 plus the use of the washer and dryer in my kitchen. Kevin was a greasy, grimy guy who sat naked on her couch covered with her blankets…ewww, yuck, disgusting! In addition, he was an idiot!

I think it's worth mentioning that Helga's home was not designed to accommodate renters. It was designed to accommodate her large family when they came to visit, so it was designed communal style. The upstairs consisted of Helga's bedroom and bath, kitchen, big living room, and office. Downstairs was my bedroom, bath, combined kitchen/laundry room, two additional bedrooms, a kitchen, a large living room, and another bathroom. With the exception of my bed and bathroom, her family had free rein of the entire house, including the washer and dryer in my kitchen. Understood. This was never a problem, because they were respectful of my space. They felt like family to me. Not so with this intruder.

I came in the kitchen one morning and heard the washer laboring to agitate, so I looked inside and could not believe anyone could be that idiotic as to load a tiny, old washer with six pairs of Levis, a large, heavy Carhartt jacket, and other miscellaneous clothes. That was his first offense. The clincher was when I went to use the washer. Opening the lid, I stood staring in astonishment when I saw that he'd washed rags that left a film of black motor oil grease inside the drum for the next person—me!

I had to tell Helga as quick as possible, so I bolted up the stairs and found her in her office where she spent about 85 percent of her time saving people from financial disaster. She was a bankruptcy attorney.

Her reply was classic Helga. Without a word, she slowly got up from her chair and walked nonchalantly downstairs to the washer to assess the damage. I was expecting her to react with the same outrage I was feeling. Instead, she opened the lid and barely looked in as she tossed a cup of detergent in, turned the water to hot, closed the lid, and went back upstairs. I stood there dumbfounded, thinking, *Really? That's it?* I ended up having to clean out the damn thing myself.

There were many occasions when he would mess up something that I'd have to fix or clean up. I hated it when people messed with my shit! That was anything that I put my time and energy into to make exactly right. Even as I'm thinking about this, I can't understand why none of these violations to her property seemed to bother her. Didn't she care about her stuff getting wrecked? I, on the other hand, took ownership of the place and cared about her things like I cared about my own. It was something I've always done.

I was becoming more resentful and angry by the minute toward Kevin with annihilation in mind for being a dumb-ass and the person who was undermining my hard work. Helga's response should have been to listen to me and do something to correct the problem. She did not. Her not stepping in felt like she was favoring him and not me, leaving me in turmoil with my feelings and issues needing to be resolved. Left to my own devices, inevitably there would be an explosion.

Two similar incidents increased my anger toward Helga for ignoring me. The last one was the worst. It began with Helga siding with Kevin the same way she took Dana's side. When that dawned on me, I felt betrayed and began yelling words to that effect at her. Without a word, she turned her back on me and made her escape up the hall stairs and away from me as I came unglued. After slamming open one of the kitchen cabinet doors, breaking it in half, I began pulling dishes and plates out of the cupboard and smashing them on the tile floor. I was incensed and out of control. Prior to this episode, I'd never felt, witnessed, or directed this kind of anger toward a friend or loved one—only with my father and stepmother, male authority figures, bosses, cops, or strangers whom I could care less about. I didn't know what my anger looked like from the receiving end.

Shortly after that incident, Helga was hosting Easter at her home with her family and wanted the entire house available. She told me I needed to find someplace to stay. She'd never done that before. I slept in my car for seven days, feeling afraid and distraught the whole time. I felt like I knew where this was headed, and I was dreading it big time.

Helga left for about month to visit family like she usually did at that time of the year. Upon her return, she brought reinforcement in the form of her long-time significant other, Jim. Within a short time, Jim delivered an eviction notice, stating when I would need to leave. I knew this was a difficult decision for Helga to make and follow through on, but that didn't deter me from wanting to make my feelings known.

I went outside and stood staring at all of my beautiful potted plants on my back porch. The thought that set things in motion was knowing Helga wouldn't take care of those plants. Coming by and seeing my once-beautiful plants suffering from neglect would upset me. Along with big, fat, huge feelings at the idea of suffering more loss, it was not something I thought I could bear. Wanting to make my protest known, I began throwing my potted plants off my patio and down the grassy slope behind the house, smashing everything to pieces.

Moving into my bedroom, I looked around at the few things I owned and thought with anguish, *I can't take anything with me except what I absolutely need.* I would be sleeping in my car—a 2002 Lexus SUV. Waves of dread crashed over and enveloped me when I tapped into the deep and familiar feelings of loss from similar experiences throughout my life. I wanted somebody to know how agonizing and traumatic it was for me to go through this again. I had no place to go! I was going to be homeless and sleeping in my car again. I was afraid I would end up homeless permanently. I was especially perplexed as to why this seemed perfectly okay with everyone.

I felt fearful, angry, and convinced my life was over as darkness began swallowing me up. I lay on my bed with these thoughts until I catapulted up and into action, grabbing things to break, things that made a loud crashing noise when making contact with the red brick patio floor outside my bedroom such as framed pictures with glass. Everything else went in the trash. Ranting out loud, I said, "I came from a middle-class family, and this is America, for God's sake! How does this happen?" I hope you understand by now how this happened to me.

The sound of glass breaking was startling, and it echoed loudly, drawing an "uh-oh" from Sara of Sara and Melissa, Helga's close friends who lived in a house below her. Sara and Jim showed up at the site where the glass was broken. We exchanged words loudly until I grabbed a handful of curtain and drew it closed.

Somewhat satisfied with the attention that stunt got me, I heard a knock on my door. It turned out to be two deputies who I slowly let in. We exchanged some words; mine were rude and obnoxious toward the younger deputy the minute he entered because he was overweight and his uniform looked terribly ill-fitting and unkempt on him. OMG! That poor unsuspecting idiot drew my attention to his appearance, which triggered my disdain and disrespect. I found it impossible to keep my mouth shut.

Well, there was no arrest, because it was not a crime to bust up my own things. The older officer knew that and said only that Helga was worried by my behavior.

I replied, "Yes, that's what Helga does!"

As the deputies are leaving, Helga appeared at my door long enough to tell me, while crying and a little hysterical, that I scared her! I don't think I believed her in that moment. After all, she wanted me out, and how did I know this wasn't a ruse to accomplish that? By then I thought she might say anything to get me to leave.

Deep feelings involving trust, betrayal, friendship, hurt, and confusion got triggered. I had trusted Helga and freaked out when she began taking measures to protect herself from me.

I was served an eviction notice by Jim that said I had two months to move out. Helga offered me $500 to move out that weekend.

I said, "That doesn't help me. I still have nowhere to go and no money."

She upped the ante to $1,000, but now she wanted everything of mine off the property.

Well, I took the offer and was out by the fifteenth. Moments before I left, Helga slid a printed paper under my door that she wanted me to sign as a part of the deal. I caught sight of the first page, one of six, declaring her free of any liability. I didn't sign it. I kicked it back under the door a time or two in astonishment and disbelief that she felt the need to do that!

As I said before, since that day, it's been nearly three years that I have been living out of my car.

"There is no greater agony than bearing an untold story inside you."

—Maya Angelou

CHAPTER 19

Mental Illness Brought Me Here

—————

've done a lot of things I'm not proud of. Shoplifting was one of those things. I shoplifted for the things I needed and couldn't pay for on and off throughout my life. Becoming a thief and stealing second nature was never a career goal. I would not have survived otherwise, nor would I have been able to maintain my addiction to booze. Being unable to keep jobs, as an addict, kept me perpetually broke and in debt to someone I inevitably couldn't pay back.

I feel such shame and embarrassment for my actions, yet tomorrow, I'll have to push those feelings aside to do it again. Nothing about being a thief is okay with me. It causes me enormous stress and turmoil, mostly because I know it grieves God and because I fear I've buried myself in a shitload of karma from which I may never be free. As a result, I've lived my life feeling disqualified from any goodness that the Universe has to offer.

It's a lot of truth to bear having lived in darkness for so long, but it needed to be brought into the light so you, the reader, can understand the full gravity of mental illness on my life. Having said that, I feel the need to apologize for being such a terrible human being. The crowd would roar, "OFF WITH HER HEAD!" and I would be deserving.

Contrasting this is the truth: deep down, I am a kind and caring person, considerate, loving (although conditional), generous, and trustworthy to those who put their trust in me. Feeling constant sadness and anger regarding my life, stealing has been a way of acting out in protest to a God I can't find when I've needed Him the most. I must have thought negative attention was better than no attention at all.

Jesus Forgives Our Sins, but Karma's a Real Bitch!

Don and I were young when we snuck upstairs into Dad's office to pilfer from the nickel slot machine. Don figured out how to break into it. Our pockets filled with nickels, we'd make our way over to the forbidden brick wall behind our home to what must have looked like the Disneyland of candy stores to a child who could buy all the candy in the world with her nickels. To be honest, I don't recall any of this happening; I just know that it did. Do you think this early experience taught me it was okay to take whatever I wanted whenever I wanted? Yep, and I believe with practice, it became a habit that I found necessary throughout my life. I've aggrieved and disappointed a number of people in my life by my choices and actions. I'm talking dear friends who truly cared about me and tried to help me succeed until, out of exasperation and bewilderment, they felt they no longer could.

Terrible Choices and Ugly Truths

Was I a bad seed from the womb? Christians would say, "Johanna, you unwittingly accepted darkness into your heart when you pocketed that first silver nickel." I knelt next to Don, who was there to support and encourage my behavior while orienting me to Five Finger Discount 101, making the whole affair special.

My therapist would say, "Johanna, you have a problem with impulse control. You have none!" My reply would be, "I'm a horrible person, and I hate what I've done! I'm finding it difficult to want to be alive."

Another scenario involved finding a box of handguns at my girlfriend's brother's house. They belonged to my girlfriend's dead father who had been a sheriff in Los Angeles county. Lori and I had been maintaining his yard for years. I spent more of my life wanting to be dead than alive, and the handgun gave me an exit plan and the illusion of being in control of my destiny. I was surprised to happen upon these guns and was immediately drawn to them. Within a second, I helped myself to what appeared to be a cop-issued 9 mm, but I later found it to be too much gun for me. I sold it to a friend who wanted it because I could use the money.

On the next visit, finding the box in the same spot, I dug around and found a smaller 22 mm handgun and grabbed it.

I expressly told my friend, "Whatever you do, DO NOT try to register the 9mm gun, as it belongs to my girlfriend's dead father." I repeated myself a few times to make sure he understood, and what does he do? All hell breaks loose when he tries to register the gun. I got a call from my girlfriend's brother, Tom, who was beside himself with shock and dismay that I would do that, and his sister did not have the inclination to see or speak to me again.

I was drinking heavily, blacking out, driving drunk, out of my mind with fear of getting caught, and not wanting to go back to jail for a third DUI, but that's exactly where I ended up for five months.

I knew what to expect, having had prior experience at the infamous hotel on the Central Coast known to the inmates as Camp Snoopy. Compared to other jails where the guards were known for their abuse of inmates, this place felt more like a preferred vacation destination that inmates looked forward to.

I needed to make sure the three things would be there when I got out: my vehicle, my German Shorthair Pointers, Jaycee and Meeko, my two loves, and my cell phone. It gave me a sense of ease to feel in control of at least the important things. I put my little Mazda truck with a camper shell in my friend's name because I couldn't leave it on the street for five months, fearing it could get towed. My dogs went with other friends. It gave me great comfort knowing these things were safe and would be there when I got out.

The friend I sold the gun to, Mike, was the same person whose name went on the pink slip to my little truck. This ended up being a huge mistake. Following the ordeal with the handgun I sold him, his anger toward me led him to sell my little truck while I was in jail for enough money to recoup the $300 he gave me for the gun.

I no longer owned a vehicle. I lost my babies as well, and I was homeless. I was sick and heartbroken.

CHAPTER 20

The Belligerent Juvenile Is Alive

T here have been many episodes of misdirected, belligerent juvenile behavior toward authority over the years. They continue to get triggered and always end badly. The next episode occurred because Melissa, of Sara and Melissa (Helga's neighbors), took steps to protect Helga from me by filing a restraining order.

Because of the list of mental health disorders, when my doctor brought up the idea that I might be bipolar, I refused to even consider it, dismissing the idea entirely. I did not want *that* disorder added to my resume of mental health illnesses, but added it was. My doctor and I experimented with mood stabilizers to address what she thought were chemical imbalances in my brain, contributing to the repeated displays of manic behavior, my BIG anger episodes. I didn't agree. One medication I tried did work to stabilize my mood. It diminished the undercurrent of agitation and negativity that has kept me in a bad mood for a long time—like a lifetime—and appears to be a precursor to the really BIG anger.

Needless to say, I was elated! My elation dissolved when I learned the medication did not touch the BIG anger at all, not even remotely. I was convinced the BIG anger was deeply rooted in the core pain and trauma from what I witnessed as a tiny child and had no control over. Talk therapy hasn't worked for me.

The process of getting the meds dialed in happens by trial and error, and so far, we have not been successful. Along with the complexities of getting the right combination of medications minus the radical and unsustainable side effects is finding therapy that worked! I've read about new methods for treating the traumatized brain, and about how trauma from childhood can get stuck in the nervous system and wreak havoc later on. In my case, the pain continues to get triggered and acted out in the present with the similar intensity of anger as experienced from the original traumatic event. I thought, *Sign me up!* As with everything else, being poor doesn't allow the privilege of that kind of care. Without question, I have a huge problem with this, and I see no solution.

Back to the Melissa story. She pulled up beside me in her white BMW SUV as I was walking down the narrow asphalt road out of the Bridgeview neighborhood to tell me that a few of the neighbors didn't like me back in the neighborhood. She said I should leave and not come back because I was on a private road.

Calmly, I stopped walking, turned to look directly at her smug face, and told her to mind her own f…king business while sporting that contorted look of "what the hell planet did you come from, you stupid moron bitch?" Cloaked in her Super Avenger Hero persona, sworn to protect, defend, and avenge all lesbians, women, small children, and animals, which included the Queen Bee of Bridgeview, Helga White, evidently.

Like a huge ominous pest in my face, I was in my head screaming, *Get the f…k away from me!* Not believing for one second that the asphalt drive was private, I said so and kept walking. I saw that she was on her cell phone as she drove past me and honked her horn, an act I took to suggest that she wasn't finished with me yet. I ignored her.

She followed me as I went to the laundromat next to the Raley's up the road. She sent the cops to talk to me and reinforce her claim that Bridgeview was a private road.

The next day, I sought out information to the contrary, much to my delight, and began plotting my next visit to Bridgeview Drive. Thoughts of getting revenge flooded in, replete with visions of specific criminal mischievousness to her person and property. The negative consequences, if I was caught, would not be worth it.

It was an abrupt invasion that interrupted me when I thought I was minding my own business, listening to music, and completely into my body with exercising being my only goal.

Yes, I wanted to screw with her for thinking where I walked was any of her business and for her superior attitude. I did go pull the sign that said Private Road out of the ground and drag it about ten feet away behind some logs and tall weeds, but in the morning, it was back. If the sun was out, I'd go back again tomorrow. Why? Because I could, and I had the law to back me, and she didn't. Maybe it was because I want to rub that reality in her dumb-ass face.

As it turned out, I did not react but backed off and thought things through. As much as I wanted to test the waters and devise a plan to mess with her, I was still on probation, and with weed, a pipe, a .38 revolver belonging to my dad, and a couple boxes of ammo in my vehicle, right or wrong about the road issue, it wouldn't matter. The cops didn't need a reason to search your vehicle when you were on probation. I'd go straight to prison. This was progress, so cheers to me!

Melissa's temporary restraining order against me was her way of keeping me off a road that passed by where I used to live and was a part of the hiking course that I trained on. Repeatedly she stated to the officers her concern for Helga's safety, leading to the altercation with the two sheriffs who attempted to serve me with it. I was scrambling to find and take my meds between interactions with sheriff number one and sheriff number two. All I could think was, *This is not right, I did not trespass on her property, and what Melissa says is a lie!!*

Officer: "She says she has a video of you."

Me: "Did you see the video?"

Officer: "No."

Me: "Let's go see Melissa's video. Come on, let's go see it. On her word you come and serve me papers without even hearing my side?"

Officer: "Tell it to the judge when you go to court."

I was indignant and mad as hell, ranting and raving, "This is so wrong!" I was extremely agitated and losing control of my anger when I threw the restraining order on the ground. I continued ranting and walked away, giving that officer enough time to drop the papers into the front passenger seat of my car through my open sunroof. I slammed open my passenger door, grabbed the papers, and threw them back at him. With both officers staring at me, I said, "I'm not taking that order! And please move your car so I can leave."

Both officers stared at me when I asked, "Am I under arrest?"

Neither officer answered, so I asked the deputy again to please move his car so I could leave. He moved his car, and I took off down the road.

I thought, *I'm certain neither sheriff will be forgetting that incident or me anytime soon.* I told you earlier that I'm a nightmare to the person who gets in my face and causes me grief, including law enforcement.

I got the impression again while hiking on the trails this morning that God wanted me to trust Him the same way I trusted Jesus with the assurance of my salvation each time I approached my hike in the woods and thought about lions. Hmmm, a deal was a deal, and I was choosing to trust that when I died, I'd spend eternity with God in his Kingdom where there is no pain and suffering, only love. Whatever happened in my life, good or bad, God kept urging me to place in his hands each situation causing me the greatest grief. Melissa, Sara, and Helga—in God's hands. SSD, my future, my inheritance from Dad's trust—in God's hands with the same confidence and assurance. I have not been successful.

Hiking had become my God time, and I used it to listen or try to. This morning, clear as day, I heard the words, "If you go back to what's comfortable, you'll die." Just when I thought I knew what that meant, I didn't. I needed to continue pondering possible meanings.

Melissa's team of Sara and Julie, another neighbor on Bridgeview Drive, won not because of their preponderance of evidence against me (they had none) but because the judge witnessed me becoming more agitated by the minute with each lie Melissa's team told. Their lies were becoming unbearable to listen to. I was wondering if everyone lied this badly in a court of law and got away with it. Melissa intentionally reiterated how badly my violent behavior scared them and said, "None of the neighbors want you in our neighborhood." Ouch!

Well, I had to put this entire ordeal in God's hands but took it back as soon as the judge made his decision to favor Melissa's request for the restraining order. He granted two years instead of five and let the gun issue go. Big score for Team Melissa.

Following the court appearance, I had time to think things through and agreed that I had no business being back in that neighborhood except that I wanted to be. I realized that I was the one who instigated the whole restraining order business.

I emailed a friend later that day, "I really am a lunatic! I lost my court case today. Do I always have to learn things the f...king hard way?"

Thinking about it later, I eased up on myself as I thought about what that neighborhood and trials around it meant to me. I was living in such isolation that I rarely ventured out. In the four years I lived in Auburn, I knew nothing about that town. When I did venture out, it was to exercise and use the training course I had always used. It was familiar and felt safe. It was the only trail I knew of to hike when it was raining as it was canopied by dense trees that kept you dry. It was the reason for being back in the area.

I can only hope that there will be a means available to deal with this horribly destructive, anger monster in me. I've impacted a lot of lives and not in a good way with each angry encounter, leaving those people wounded and scared.

Another episode occurred when Melissa called in a bogus complaint that I was in the neighborhood on Bridgeview again. She told the cops I had a gun in my car, and that she and her partner, Sara were afraid for their safety.

The scene unfolded in public with me refusing to let this extremely determined officer search my vehicle. After all, it was my right! While I was feeling mildly smug about my victory, the officer told me to turn around and put my hands on the wall of the adjacent Bank of America. In stunned protest at the wrongness of what was happening, I began backing away and refused to let this happen. I was being chased around a large trash container when he caught my arm and swung me around and then face first onto the concrete.

I recall sitting in the back seat of the sheriff's cruiser, handcuffed, with a stern and serious deputy looking directly into my eyes, shouting at me three times to "Grow up!" He told me, "Have some respect!"

I recognized why I did not. What came to me when I saw myself through the eyes of the deputy was a sixty-two-year-old woman behaving like a belligerent juvenile delinquent, professing, "I didn't do it, and she's deliberately lying to get me in trouble. I didn't do a thing, and I'm the one being punished!? It's not fair!"

These are reenactments of scenarios involving a sibling (my brother, most likely), and they continue to play out in the present when certain emotions get triggered. I don't remember anything, but it must have involved my dad or my mom, maybe even an uncle that I'm still angry at, not the poor cop paid to do his job. This is a huge part of my anger, my volatile reaction toward authority. My anger has caused the most trouble in my life.

A couple months prior, I took my father's gun to a pawn shop and sold it. I had mixed feelings about it as it was the only thing I had left of him after he passed, and I couldn't seem to give it up. I had perjured myself the last time I was in court with Melissa and Sara, as I declared I did not own a gun when they said I did. That's why they sicced the cops on me. I got away with it. A part of me knew I should not have a gun at all, ever, but I couldn't part with it until my need for money collided with my desire to keep it. Money won out. If it came up stolen, I could be in trouble for violating probation, at which point I would not pass go or collect $200. I would go straight to Alcatraz where they'd leave me on that great big rock to rot and not tell a soul.

As it happened, Dad and Kathleen (his third wife) were out one evening when I began snooping, and I found the loaded .38 revolver when I opened the drawer of my father's nightstand. My dad was in the late stages of alcohol-related dementia, and a loaded handgun was the last thing that should be in that drawer. I was stupefied. Bringing the issue of the gun up that evening, I told her she needed to take it to the police, and she said she would. She didn't but told me she did. Weeks later when I found the gun still in his drawer, I took it, had it cleaned, stored in a locked gun case, and put it somewhere safe: with me. Several weeks had gone by before Kathleen called to ask me if I had taken the gun. I said no. I know, I know, I'm going to hell, but she lied first. She said, "I guess I'll need to report it to the police as stolen."

I said, "It's probably a good idea" and hung up.

So far, no one has come looking for me. I would think they'd be happy I got rid of it, right?

CHAPTER 21

Sweet Vindication

My attorney won my SSD case that was filed four years earlier. It's been six months, and I haven't seen a dime of back pay yet. It will be something, but it won't be enough to make a difference. Not enough to make a lifestyle change, which is what I desperately need. This waiting feels unbearable.

Vindication soothes the soul of the pain and shame inflicted by a world without understanding of what mental health illness looks like or how the sufferer is impacted.

I just learned that I won't be getting my money for another month. I've been lying low and trying to be patient. More like I'm staying high because I am not jubilant.

I'm alone out on the trail. Stopping, I look up through the sparse branches of oak leaves for shade and find little. Acknowledging how alone I am in this life, I ask myself how I've gotten so far away from society to end up this alone. I don't want to be alone, but alone I am, and it makes me feel like an incredibly strange person in a strange land.

I'm not feeling enthusiastic about continuing life at sixty-two years old if nothing changes. What kind of life am I going to have? I have no family, no community, no roots, no tribe, no partner, no money, and no true friends who haven't been scared off by what they don't understand. Truly, it's just me, my lonesome self, tumbling down the road like a kicked can going nowhere and anywhere far from anything resembling a home.

I have lived a rotten stinking life, always feeling like a misfit, awkward, and tentative interacting with others. I didn't know how to get involved with others, groups of people, athletic teams, etc. Appearing cool and unfazed, I resigned myself to a position on the outside looking in, but in reality, I longed to be on the inside.

I may have started retreating from people at that point and turned my attention toward myself through health and fitness, exercise, and riding my motorcycle. I've been retreating ever since, but worse, the shame I've felt for feeling like such a failure and disappointment has propelled me even farther away from people. My world would grow smaller over time because of the impact mental illness has had on my inability to keep a job.

Three years earlier, my friend DeDe, from back in my motocross days, managed to track me down from the aborted attempts at starting but never completing a Facebook homepage. I had been missing in action for about forty years when I was found in full survival mode by DeDe and then my MX community and high school classmates. Making that connection with people I felt cared about me drew me back into existence, like a breath of life, with praise for my accomplishments and contributions as a racer chick in Women's Professional Motocross from the seventies. I had no idea I had been viewed in that light. It was a huge surprise to be referred to as a legend, hero, pioneer, and champion.

CHAPTER 22

The Step-Monster from Hell!

Well, there's always one of these psycho types who thrive on drama in every movie involving money, power, scandal, and deception. Mine is a witch named Kathleen. On several occasions when Kathleen was unable to keep a bizarre alter ego tapped down, I watched as it bared its fangs, hissed, and snarled. I've witnessed the physical transformation facially—eyes bulging out like those of House Speaker Nancy Pelosi when seen in an image on Facebook being likened to the most evil and despicable humans on the planet. I was startled when Pelosi's image appeared on the TV screen because the resemblance to Kathleen is uncanny.

OMG! I saw the same bulging eyeballs on Kathleen when speaking lies and contradictions while yelling at my dad, telling him he didn't know what he was talking about (whenever there was any mention of the trust) and to shut up! The reason she wants to keep the amount of money a mystery has me concerned, but there is nothing I can do to change anything. If I had the money, I'd hire an attorney. For whatever the reason, she needs to have complete control and is willing to lie, cheat, and steal to keep control, as she is the Grand Madam of Deceit!

Women like Kathleen live to screw with the lives of others so they themselves can feel powerful. This causes me to wonder what kind of trauma she experienced as a child to be the way she is or whether she is the devil incarnate, sent to seek and destroy me.

Presently, Kathleen is holding my father's trust money hostage because she can. She can do whatever the hell she wants, because like the last wife, she managed to gain my father's emotional trust and control of the financial trust before he passed. Women like Kathleen and Dottie are intelligent, clever, manipulative, and devious. I'm going to go so far as to say diabolical. These two women came with an agenda to make themselves indispensable in some way that served my father with their sights set on gaining money, power, and security.

A short time after my father's death, I called Kathleen to check in on her. During our brief chat, she asked me if I wanted to be put in charge of the trust and added to their bank account. Sensing something was up, I tentatively said, "Yes, I guess, if that's what you want."

I made the eight-hour trip down to Southern California to get things arranged. I showed up at Kathleen's house, giving her about a thirty-minute heads-up that I'd be there. After the usual chitchat, I asked her to contact her attorney and get down to business. Well, I witnessed Kathleen pretending to call her attorney and ask questions. As she hung up the phone, she directed her attention back to me and said, "It isn't something that can be changed without your father's signature." She already knew this, and now she knew I knew this and knew she was so busted! She shrugged it off like that never happened.

I was so upset that I didn't talk to her the entire evening. Before the sun came up the following morning, I was out the door and headed home. Each of us had been pretending to like the other for obvious reasons, and I never trusted her. Once my father was out of the picture, boy oh boy did she show her true colors. Yikes!!

It was about a week and a half before I called her again. As soon as I said, "Hello Kathleen," I was hit in the face with this fabricated barrage of accusations. "Oh don't you Kathleen me!" and "You know damn well what I'm talking about!"

With my mind racing back and forth, searching for any truth in what she was saying and finding none, I exclaimed, "What!?" My voice climbed an octave with my reply, "What are you talking about, Kathleen?"

"You came here, took what you wanted, and disappeared. You took the original, and I reported it stolen to the police."

I had that sinking feeling in my gut and thought, *What the f...k is she talking about? What kind of game is she playing now?*

She said, "You are no longer welcome in my home" and hung up.

Looking upward, in a pleading voice, I said, "Please, God, don't let this be happening!"

A year and a half went by, and Kathleen still wouldn't answer her phone. I had been broke going into the fourth year waiting for a determination on my disability case. I hocked everything I owned of value to survive. When I got some money, I headed straight down to see what this crazy witch was up to.

I parked outside the mobile home park on the street in case I needed to make a quick get-away and quickly walked in. My heartbeat picked up as I approached what felt like enemy territory. The perfectionist in me was noticing all the little things that needed to be fixed around the place, and I thought, *You really are sick!* I was thinking about all the different ways this could go wrong, and then up the short steps I went. I knocked on her door. When she opened it and our eyes connected, I saw reluctant approval telling me to enter. As I did, I felt slightly relieved and pleasantly surprised she did that. That feeling dissolved the instant she responded to my question. "Kathleen, what's going on? You don't answer your phone in over a year, you haven't responded to my written correspondence, and with this COVID thing going on, for all I know, you could be dead and rotting in this place!!"

With her voice rising and eyeballs bulging out of their sockets, she shouted back, "Now you've seen me. Get the hell out!"

I said, "No! I want to know what's going on! You know my situation. I've asked for help, and you ignored me, but you're giving money to Dana (my sister) and Lori (her daughter) and not to me. Why are you punishing me! What did I do to you?" I couldn't think of a thing.

She shouted, "I don't have to tell you a goddamn thing!"

I said, "Oh yes, you do! Aren't you supposed to be, like, my stepmother or something!? Instead, you're being a cruel bitch, and you're not honoring my dad's wishes."

"I don't have to tell you a goddamn thing. Now get out of my house!"

"No!"

She went to pick up the receiver to call the police, fumbled with it, and it fell next to her. Lunging forward and with lightning-fast reflexes, I grabbed the phone before she could, stood up, and stepped back, holding the phone above her head, just out of reach, playfully taunting her with it and enjoying the heck out of it!

"Uh-oh! Now what are you gonna do, Kathleen? It's not fun to feel out of control, is it?"

The look she gave me was so worth seeing. It was the look of surprise and panic when she realized she'd lost control of her 911 lifeline. Otherwise, she showed no emotion. At that point, I felt compelled to ask her if she was Satan.

She didn't reply, just stared back expressionless, with a blank look and dull eyes. When she was able to find another phone, she called the police. I turned on my heel and made haste to get out of there, but I still had the phone in my hand when I got outside. Wiping it clean of my fingerprints, I turned back, opened the door, tossed the phone back in, and was out of there.

As I was driving off, here came the sheriff headed toward me. I thought about the horrors she could concoct about me and get away with because she was such a convincing liar. I was glad to be driving home and not to jail. That was the last time I saw Kathleen.

On a previous occasion, I was in a verbal altercation with my father one afternoon while I was back in my hometown, San Clemente, when Kathleen entered the scene and decided she was going to get in my face, poking her finger at me and telling me what a piece of shit I was. I told her to get away from me and gave her a slight little push.

Scene two: The actor appears and stumbles back a few steps. As though watching a movie in slow motion, she went into a staggering, backward decent and landed on one knee. Holding her elbow up to get my father's attention without so much as a scratch on any part of her body, she said, "Don, what are you going to do?"

"Well," he said, "have her arrested!"

Not wanting any part of that, I jogged to my vehicle, got in, and put it in reverse to back up.

Enter my brother, Don, who pulled up behind me and pinned me in. I got out of my car and went to his driver door as he was getting out and kicked his door closed on him. Bad idea! When he managed to get out, he reared back and punched me in the jaw (though not hard), threw me on the ground, and sat on me while declaring he was making a citizen's arrest. "You're going down, little sister, you're going down!

My brother was a huge beast of a dude, weighing close to 250 pounds at the time. I couldn't move or breathe. I was flattened like a bug squashed under foot, face down on the concrete with zero wiggle room to attempt an escape. I was seeing stars, going in and out of darkness...

There was the animosity that had continued to grow over the years unabated. Evidently, he'd been waiting a long time to "take me down." I'm sure he celebrated that victory that afternoon with unabashed glee.

Meanwhile, the sheriff was collecting witness statements as my family conspired to throw me under the bus, claiming that Kathleen was afraid for her life, blah, blah, blah. I was charged with assault and battery and went straight to jail. I did not pass go or collect $200. I spent five days in Orange County Jail while my Capitalise German Shorthair Pointers, my babies and companions who traveled with me, spent five days in lockup at the local dog pound. My vehicle was impounded.

I was so shocked and hurt by the way "my family" treated me that day, I didn't speak to my father for seven years. The scary discovery I wish I hadn't made that day was seeing the power Kathleen had over my father. She instigated and orchestrated that entire drama, and it was her influence that demanded I be criminally charged and thrown in jail. My father stood there looking like he didn't know what to feel or say and was going along with her for the ride. Acquiescing to this strong female figure the same way he did with his dominant, exacting mother was a visible exchange of power. It was a startling observation and the first incident where the scary witch alter ego appeared, making sure I understood who was in charge. I knew I was screwed!

As I was trying to flee my Twilight Zone, I blurted words to the effect that I would come back and strangle her in her sleep! This was warfare with an enemy whose game was not familiar. While acknowledging defeat, I needed a damaging last blow on my way out. Unmedicated and unfiltered, stuff like this shot from my smart mouth without warning or thought as to the consequences, and it always made matters worse. I call this mania madness, being in my mental manic state. It can be different levels of scary for different people.

Seven years later, out of nowhere came a check in the mail for $1,000, like a carrot on a string, and a note asking me to bury the hatchet and come see my dad, because he was getting up there in age. Well, I wanted to see my dad, but unfortunately, he and Kathleen were a package deal.

I don't know that I'll ever bury the hatchet where Kathleen is concerned, but I do know where I'd like it buried.

Why are these women in my life causing me grief? Universe, what have I done to deserve more loss and more suffering? Haven't I suffered enough?

CHAPTER 23

As a Matter of Fact

Fact: Female Professional Motocross Pioneer and Legend of the seventies, Johanna Stenersen, was the winner of two 250 cc National Titles in Women's Professional Motocross (1976 and 1977), District 37 #1 plate (1975), and two-time winner of the Classic Mammoth Mountain Motocross (1975 and 1976).

Fact: Johanna Stenersen, Southern California, and Sue Fish, LA County, met for the first time in 1975 at Carlsbad Raceway, D-37 Motocross. Johanna won. Over the next three years, Johanna and Sue were inseparable on and off the racetrack, dominating the field of Women's MX while elevating the sport to new levels and giving young girls something to aspire to.

Political Bullshit with a Load of Deception and Scandal

Unfortunately, the AMA (American Motorcycle Association) and governing body over all things having to do with the motorcycle racing industry, had someone in their ranks who wanted to sabotage the history of Women's Professional Motocross and eliminate my involvement entirely. Someone wanted to make it all about little Suzy

Fish—girl next door, charming, funny, and deserving of the recognition she earned for her efforts to elevate Women's Pro Motocross, something neither she nor I could have accomplished without the other at that time. I was cheated out of my share of recognition and eliminated entirely from the annals of the AMA. Why, you ask? Obviously, it was to promote little Suzy Fish as THE dominant Female Pro MXer of the seventies and worthy of AMA's Hall of Fame.

Ghost Legend

I was dumbfounded when I learned that I was not mentioned among the other women recognized for their contribution to the sport of Women's MX as a Legend, Pioneer, Champion, or Hero. Anyone who spent time around motocross tracks in the mid-seventies would know it wasn't all about Sue Fish—not to take anything away from Sue, as she got her due recognition. Sue and I were best friends and fiercest rivals. The mid to late seventies was "our" era, and our battles were EPIC!! Sue kicked my butt as much as I kicked hers.

Again, you ask, why wasn't I mentioned? A slightly more devious reason will become clear as I take you back to the evening Sue and I came close to exchanging blows and haven't seen or spoken to one another since. It's been twenty years.

First, here are some comments made by witnesses, people who were actually at our races. The following statements were instrumental in loving me back into existence from a forty-year-long journey from hell.

Debbie Matthews: "I loved watching you two go at it. You brought out the best in each other, elevating and enriching the sport. You were fast and furious, feminine warriors giving me and the industry something to aspire to become. Thank you for bringing Women's Motocross to the next level and doing it with style."

Dee Granger Ritter: "I remember all the spectators lining the fences to see Johanna Stenersen and Sue Fish dice it out with ferocity and passion! Female warriors indeed! And yes, you two and all who raced their friends behind you (and were lapped by you!) are what made the women's division such a success! They were the glory days for most of us!"

Debbie Matthews: "Both your comments were right on target. We all are so privileged to have lived and been part of the birth of women's moto. Which wonderful memories and friendships."

Joe Miller: "Thanks for the recent add, Johanna. I grew up in So Cal like a lot of you here and in doing so attended and participated in, let's say, a lot of motorcycle races over the last fifty-five or so years. Mostly with my pop who was involved in races a couple years before I dropped in...Anyway, I believe his favorite memory (as he told the story often) was of the many moto races he saw with you and Sue Fish going tooth and nail lap after lap in a most unreal fashion. He was totally amazed at the level of competition you two exhibited. With that being said, I think if he were still here today, he'd be giving you a standing ovation on this honor. Congrats Johanna!"

Laurra Maddock: "You two were so awesome…so glad I was around to see and appreciate firsthand how good you two were. You and Sue raised women's racing to a new level. If you didn't have each other to compete against, it wouldn't have had the same effect."

Gale Webb: "Laura couldn't have said it better than that. I also couldn't wait to watch you girl's race!! You were ahead of and made women's racing what it is today. So much respect to you. YOU WILL ALYAYS BE OUR HEROS."

Laurra Maddock: "If you and Sue were in the race, and if both of you finished, everyone else was racing for third place. It shouldn't be about what trophies were won, it should be about racing ability, and how the people participating in the sport molded the sport and directed its growth. We're not THAT old—we're still alive…anyone writing about women's MX history HAS to TALK TO the people who were there. If they did, they would include both you and Sue from the seventies. This is when it went from putt-putt Powder Puff to real racing. You and Sue were instrumental in creating that change. The two of you were so good it was scary. The two of you put the MX world on notice that women rock!"

Dan Murphy: "I was there…I loved watching you battle with Sue and the other gals. You were absolutely a force to be reckoned with and should be recognized for your efforts."

Curt Evans: "Johanna's the real deal."

Jack Wright: "Johanna Stenersen and Sue Fish pushed each other forward. The competition between them raised each (and women's MX) to greater and greater levels. You can't separate the two names."

Mike Johns: "Johanna, I was racing near Tucson today, and I had one of the kids from my summer MX camps come over to see me. She's a thirteen-year-old girl who is just starting racing. I shared your Facebook page with her and Sue's too. I told her the stories of the most ferocious, epic battles between you two and how you both today are legends of our sport. She was awed by you! She made the comment that she wanted to be just like you."

Mike Johns: "You earned it...we 'fans' just marvel at what you gals did and try to find someone to listen to the stories!!! You wrote the chapters; we share the tales to the new generations of riders..."

Joe Miller: "What I mentioned above tells it all. You two were in a class by yourself."

Allen Cooke: "Well, Johanna Stenersen, as you well know, I was there through most of those days, and I have a great memory of those days, even after landing on my head so many times, and still do, I just don't get up as quick. I've seen a lot of great battles in the women's class starting in 1970, but I must say that your speed and talent was not matched by many, and your battles with Sue Fish were epic."

This is hardly "powder puff" racing — Fish (left) and Stenerson were within shouting distance of each other all day.

In the Women's Pro class, the battle between Sue Fish and Johanna Stenersen raged on, with Johanna taking home the top bucks for the day with a 1-2-1 finishing record.   Heidbrink photo

Johanna Stenerson led Sue Fish in the 250 class. Johanna won, but Sue took the title.

Johanna Stenersen

JOHANNA STENERSEN,
Carlsbad Raceway 1975

1976 Women's Nationals
San Antonio, Texas

June 22, 1977 **CYCLE NEWS**

Johanna Stenerson holeshot every moto in both 125cc and 250cc classes at the Women's championship.

JOHANNA STENERSEN,
D-37 # 1 plate, Women's Expert 1976

JOHANNA (top) SUE (bottom) 1975;
JOHANNA STENERSEN, Saddleback Park 1977.

Cherry Stockton and Johanna Stenerson smile at the photographer while Johanna's boyfriend takes a pic. Heldbrink photo.

Women's Standings

DISTRICT 37 WOMEN'S DIV.
MOTO-X 1st QUARTER STANDING

1.Johanna Stenerson	178.2
2.Lori Payne	170.5
3.Cheryl Acres	162.8
4.Nancy Payne	90.0
5.Roberta Vasilis	77.0
6.Charleen Higgins	76.0
7.Gale Webb	73.0
8.Linda Stinebaugh	65.0
9.Sue Fish	64.8
10.Paulette Neeofeene	61.9
11.Denise deVines Beardshear	52.0
12.Marcia Holley	51.7
13.Juliann Vasilis	49.5
14.Cherry Stockton	48.0
15.Denise Duncan	48.0
16.Sue Hall	45.0
17.Dianne Connolly	42.9
18.Kim Byers	33.0
19.Dee Grander	31.0
20.Robin C. Sauls	30.0
21.Jeanette Linden	28.0
22.Mickey Phillips	28.0
23.Thelma Lou	20.0
24.Chelle Blythe	20.0
25.Linda McNamara	18.0
26.Karen Traw	11.0
27.Lisa Downhill	5.0

Even off the track, Sue and Johanna fool around on Sue's XR special. She is fast on a mini too.

CHAPTER 24

Gone Fishing

t was the summer of 2001 when I went to live with my friend Sue Fish—personal trainer, athlete, outdoors woman, etc.

I was living in my father's thirty-two-foot motorhome on his commercial property in San Clemente, drinking myself stupid, and so miserable. About that time, I took a job across the street at a Chinese American fast-food restaurant, Pick Up Stix. Remember, I didn't understand the extent of my mental illnesses or how they undermined my life, especially my ability to keep a job. I thought it was my bad attitude and dislike for demanding people.

Well, it didn't take long to figure out that Pick Up Stix and I were, once again, not a good fit. The first time I was thrown on the computer and told to take phone orders, I couldn't keep up. I wasn't confident enough on the computer to be thrown in on a lunch shift. I remember becoming extremely anxious and confused as it seemed like the people calling in phone orders were speaking Japanese. I got panicky and angry. Anger was my default emotion. Anger was directly where I went the instant I felt fear or shame.

There was a strong undercurrent of fear of failure and shame for not working quickly enough. In short, I ended up in the cooler with my manager, him yelling at me and me yelling back at him for getting upset with me. The beginning of the lunch shift saw my backside slamming through the glass front doors without a backward glance. It should be obvious by now that I do not take criticism well.

Sue and I were chatting it up on the phone quite a bit, stopping on occasion long enough to run out for another bottle of wine. I was desperate for change and to get away from my sick-ass family. Sue invited me to come live with her in Santa Barbara. She also gave me encouragement and support to get back into massage therapy, something I loved to do and was good at. Some years back, I made another impulsive decision to sell my table. I wanted to go back to school, and somehow, in my black-and-white thinking, I couldn't do both. Come to find out later, it would have been the ideal job to have to work around a school schedule. Not having a table had me feeling unsure that this plan would sail.

Sue added, "You'll have a ready-made clientele," meaning she would send some of her wealthy Montecito clients my way to get me started. "Just get up here, and we'll figure out the table situation later."

Back when we first met, Sue was a senior in high school at Monterey Park. After being kicked out of San Clemente High the beginning of my senior year, I graduated from San Clemente Adult School in 1976. I was seventeen and graduated a year behind my class of '75. Mom died during my senior year, and I went off the rails emotionally, making a point of acting out in true belligerent, juvenile delinquent form. Getting a hug or being held and comforted during this time would have gone a long way to defuse the ticking time bomb I had become. Yeah, I'm pretty sure some love would have fixed a few things.

I was looking forward to hanging with my friend and enjoying some adventures in hiking, biking, and other fun outdoor stuff together. Sue and I liked doing the same kind of things, which I found to be rare. Throw a little competitive spirit in, and it became that much more fun.

One summer evening, we had been arguing and met briefly in the hallway upstairs in Sue's house. Sue abruptly declared, "Do you know what your problem is?"

I thought, *Do tell.*

"You have always followed in my shadow!"

Astounded, I said, "What?? Are you kidding me, you f… king narcissist!! It's always about you, Fish, isn't it?"

At this point, we were in each other's face. Sue reared back with her hand balled in a fist suspended in midair, shaking. She was so furious as my mouth was going off, egging her on. I don't remember how we managed to part ways without incident. Thankfully, she had some restraint, because one good punch would have sent "Alice to the moon!"

True to her word, Sue began funneling clients my way. A vivid and unforgettable incident that occurred one Sunday afternoon epitomizes the extent to which I was drinking and creating episodes.

The day before, a client called to book two massage appointments: one for herself and one for her husband outside on their wooden deck off the back of their beautiful home. It was a treat to work on clients outdoors in the fresh air and sunshine. Add the wonderful elements from nature, and the senses came alive, wanting to absorb everything to enhance the experience. Their backyard was the perfect place for that.

Around the time of their appointments that Sunday, I got a call from the clients, asking why I wasn't there. Any excuse would sound lame at this point, and we all knew it. Sue and I had partied way too much, and I couldn't recall having the conversation the day before because I was blackout drunk.

The drinking had already begun that Sunday, and no way was I going to show up late and drunk. I needed to come up with an excuse. These people were professionals (doctors, I believe) who scheduled their lives and the lives of their four children around the massage appointments that obviously were of considerable importance to them. They would not be booking any massages with me in the future.

I knew I had f...ked up and was in big trouble with booze, again, and my life was out of control. As usual, there was nothing I could to about it except run.

Driving north to anywhere and nowhere, I was thinking about what had just happened between Sue and me. I picked up my cell phone and called her to say, "I'm so sorry this happened. We were in our addictions. We're alcoholics!" I told her I loved her and hung up.

Sue didn't say a word, but in her silence, there was a strong undercurrent of emotion stirring just beneath the surface like a witch's brew of anger, resentment, and disappointment.

I felt resentment toward Sue for not being the friend and inspiration I had hoped for, as I'm sure Sue had her expectations and disappointments about me. As I mentioned earlier, I was looking forward to hanging out with my friend and having some fun being physically active and outdoors. I'd gotten away from my healthy lifestyle and exchanged it for misery and inactivity, hoping to obliterate myself with booze because I hated my life.

As one might guess, that didn't happen. Instead, it turned into a classic case of the blind leading the blind. We became each other's partner in crime and encouragement to party on. Sue was swallowing pain pills like M&Ms, having suffered numerous crashes and broken bones from racing. I know this because I was there at the race with her when she crashed her 1200 cc Kawasaki sports bike at Willow Springs. The trip to the hospital and conversation centered around Sue Fish again!

Several weeks later, Sue crashed a client's borrowed street bike in a collision involving another vehicle. The first thing I asked was if she had been on medication at the time. Her reply was that she hadn't. Well, I wasn't buying it. In my experience with narcotic pain medications, I know how easy it was to overuse and abuse them, and if you were an addict, well, that was a given. Mixed with alcohol and consumed over an extended period, there was going be a residual effect on the body's cells, tissues, and every organ including the brain and nervous system that will affect timing, coordination, reflexes, etc. You can't ride a motorcycle without giving 110 percent of your attention and focus to riding. Having been both an athlete and motorcycle racer, Sue knew this but wasn't taking any heed. Instead, she thought I was jealous and trying to discourage her from pursuing her passion.

She turned to me and asked in a challenging way, "What are you passionate about?" Well, I knew the answer was nothing, but that wasn't the point! I was trying to discourage her from killing herself, because living friends were more fun to play with.

A Fish's Tale

I didn't know Sue's thoughts and feelings over the next twenty years until I heard through the MX grapevine, several years after the 2014 Women's Celebration of MX History, that she was telling her tale.

I set out to find answers from my motocross friends from back in the day, other women who ran in the same races with Sue and me for three years. No one made mention of that happening. What did get mentioned was that I "took advantage of Sue's kindness and generosity."

People who were friends with both of us seemed cautious and unwilling to dish out any helpful information, gossip or truth. When I completed my fishing expedition, it seemed I was the only one left in the dark. It felt like there was a force field around Sue, protecting the image the AMA, had built her up as "THE female Pro MX racer of the seventies who single-handedly dominated the field of pro women racers." With no one talking, it felt ridiculously like a conspiracy. What for? So Fish could have the limelight all to herself? Why did it need to be at my expense?

Reflecting back twenty years and based on my track history, I will concede that yes, I am guilty as charged for taking advantage of my friend, but nobody sets out intentionally to hurt the people they love. I didn't. At that point in my life, my alcoholism was in full regalia. I was doing what an alcoholic does best when running from God and her demons: drink to excess, make terrible choices, and leave casualties behind in the wake of her internal war. I'm sorry that happened. If I could have made better choices, I would have.

I landed back in San Luis Obispo while my alcoholism continued unabated and accelerated over the next seven years, becoming some of the most self-destructive and costly years of my life.

Well, behind the scenes, someone took to heart Sue's cause and made certain I would pay for my crime, using the occasion of the History of Women's Motocross to make me disappear. Did my crime warrant a personal attack that cheated me out of the acknowledgment and celebration of the best years of my life?

I can only believe Sue had to know what was going on and was careful to stay clear of any appearance of being involved. Instead, what I found was a female race promoter named Tami with close ties to the AMA and a reputation for being disreputable. She was the person who appeared to be behind the articles, so I started there.

I conversed with Tami by email. It bores me to repeat the obvious silly lies she told me, one after another. When she put the blame on the research team at AMA or the female race promotor back in the seventies when I was racing, she couldn't backpedal out of that lie if she tried. Stupid girl! I knew the race promotor, Kasey Rogers, back then. Kasey was the first one to recognized Sue's and my speed and talent by witnessing our epic battles on the track firsthand. It also became the first time women were classified as pros and made a little money. "We" were credited with elevating the sport to a higher level by Kasey Rogers.

I hope for the chance to have a face to face someday with Tami, the "good friend" of Sue Fish and behind-the-scenes person who was able to manipulate circumstances to promote her agenda. I'd ask her why she felt the need to stick her nose where it wasn't needed. Sue already received the Number One title and recognition as a Hall of Fame inductee on her own merit. I'd want to know if revenge was her motivation, you know, sympathy revenge on Sue's behalf.

Knowing I had no interest in hearing a single word from her lying lips, I indulged my dark imagination to dispose of her. What this would look like involved tearing her ass from limb to limb, stuffing it piece by piece into a wood-chipper, and enjoying watching it spray red.

As for Sue Fish? I'm sorry it's been twenty years and that we are unable to resolve our differences, as I have missed my friend.

Congratulations on all your accomplishments, Sue, and for the recognition you always dreamed of having. As for me, struggling with mental illness didn't allow me to dream dreams. For the record, had I continued racing and had the same network of support as you, you would be "following in my shadow!" We were into racing motorcycles for different reasons.

Heal Your Pain, Heal Your Life

That was then, and this is now. The only goals I have are to find healing, make peace with my demons, and be happy awhile. Who knows…maybe I'll run into my authentic persona and get to know her? In the meantime, I'm staying high because I'm not too f..king jubilant!

I sincerely hope there's a purpose in all of this and that something good comes from it. Otherwise, the last sixty-two years will have been a complete waste of a life that had all the potential in the world to be anything at all. I truly believe I would have been unstoppable!

Instead, as fate would have it, I was cursed from the gate and destined for doom. My story is a clear and convincing message of an innocent life stolen by alcoholism and domestic violence.

ALCOHOLISM
AND
DOMESTIC VIOLENCE

EQUAL
DAMAGED CHILDREN,
MENTAL ILLNESS,
POVERTY,
CRIMINALITY,
PRISON,
AND
DEATH
WHAT A TRAGIC LEGACY
TO LEAVE
ANOTHER INNOCENT HUMAN LIFE!!

Finally, the biggest roadblock to healing and transformation for me has been finding the kind of treatment that leads to real healing. Having limited resources has made this search impossible thus far. Maybe this is what is meant in the message I received earlier, urging me to press forward and not give up on finding help that heals or I would die. Living in my own private hell the past forty years feels like I'm already dead, so what's the difference?

Maybe it's finally understanding that I've made a huge mess of things that can't be fixed on my own, and I need God's help. You have to know that admitting defeat stinks! Fear not—being the prodigal daughter that I am, I know home is the place to go where they can't turn you away. Since I have no more brilliant choices, I'll run to the Father and fall into grace. Failing that, I am not above pleading guilty by reason of insanity!

Holy Father, I lay all that I am at your feet and choose to believe you have my back. I have to trust in your plan for my life, as I clearly have no other choices, and I will believe, because I need to be your miracle!

Lastly, my deepest apologies to those of you who had the misfortunate of crossing paths with me and adversely impacted. Apologies don't cut it sometimes, but there it is... And a special thanx to all of you who took the time to read my story, and for your kind and generous support which made publishing this story possible...

Much love and appreciation,

Johanna

Made in the USA
Monee, IL
15 November 2021